Wings Across the Desert

Wings Across the Desert

THE INCREDIBLE MOTORIZED CRANE MIGRATION

WILDLIFE ODYSSEY: BOOK I

David H. Ellis

hancock

house

ISBN 0-88839-480-2
Copyright © 2001 David H. Ellis

Cataloging in Publication Data
Ellis, David H. 1945–
Wings across the desert

Includes bibliographical references.
ISBN 0-88839-480-2

1. Sandhill crane—Migration—Arizona. 2. Sandhill crane
—Training—Arizona. I. Title.
QL696.G84E34 2001   598.3'2   C00-910826-2

Printed in Canada—PRINTCRAFTERS

Editor: Ruth McVeigh
Production and cover design: Ingrid Luters
Front cover photograph: David H. Ellis
Back cover photographs: David H. Ellis (top), Jim Lish (bottom)

Chapter heading vignette photo: Mary Bishop
Line drawings: Billi Wagner

Published simultaneously in Canada and the United States by

HANCOCK HOUSE PUBLISHERS LTD.
19313 Zero Avenue, Surrey, B.C. V3S 9R9

HANCOCK HOUSE PUBLISHERS
1431 Harrison Avenue, Blaine, WA 98230-5005

(604) 538-1114   Fax (604) 538-2262
(800) 938-1114   Fax (800) 983-2262
Web Site: www.hancockhouse.com   email: sales@hancockhouse.com

Contents

Preface

An old Arab proverb reads: "A story worth telling is worth embellishing." When writing fiction or even an historical novel, the whole story is embellishment, but when describing actual events, as I do in this book, a strict adherence to the truth is imperative. Contemporary English literature is awash in fantasy. And if fantasy is your fare, read no further. But if you suspect, as I know, that truth is very often stranger than and always more memorable than fiction, perhaps you will discover what you seek in these pages. In what follows, I have tried to tell as accurately as possible the tale of our 1995 and 1996 truck-led crane migrations.

Having proclaimed my intent to tell only the truth, I must now qualify my statement. Many quotations in this book are reconstructed from imperfectly remembered dialogue; many are directly from journal entries, while a few represent clear memories, with much of the dialogue reconstructed from the general flow of remembered conversations. Some descriptive details are best guesses. For example, I really am not sure if the rockhound we queried about our lost cranes on October 7 was missing his left or his right medial incisor. With the goal of improving accuracy, almost every episode has been read by some or all participants. One name (i.e., I use John Punchcow) has been changed to avoid embarrassing family members and to stave off law suits.

Although this volume really reports two separate, year apart, migrations (ten cranes in 1995 and twelve in 1996), I have collated the anecdotes from the two years into one migration, to speed up the narrative. I take license for so doing from literary need and from John Wesley Powell's example. When Powell published his epic volume on the first explorations of the Grand Canyon and its tributaries, he did just as I have done; he presented happenings in upstream to downstream order, regardless of year.

In late May, a quiet, gurgling chirp is heard from a large obovate egg. A day later, a tiny chip appears on the surface. The calls are now louder. The bird struggles in its narrow confinement. As the hours pass,

Crane chick ready to hatch. *Drawing by Kate Spencer*

she enlarges the hole into a jagged line circling the large end of the egg. After 30 hours, the struggle is over and a greater sandhill crane chick emerges . . . ready for training, a slate ready, even anxious, to be written upon. This book tells the story of the twenty-eight chicks that were selected to be trained to enter and ride in an army ambulance, and of the twenty-five that were transported from their rearing site at Patuxent Wildlife Research Center in Maryland to a reintroduction site located within the former breeding range of the sandhill crane in northern Arizona. Only one colt died during shipment and the remaining 24 survived five weeks of flight training. Of these, 22 began the migration, flapping their way south behind the army ambulance, flying nearly 400 miles to a wintering area on the Mexican border.

The tedium of daily life training the chicks, the dangers to the birds and our research team during the migration, the humorous episodes, the euphoric highs when we were on the road with our cranes in formation, bravely flapping in tow, the anxiety and emotional nadirs we experienced after eagle attacks and other losses: these form the substance of this little volume.

What purpose was there in training sandhill cranes to follow a truck? Simply put, to help save the whooper. There is only one self-sustaining wild population of whooping cranes. It currently consists of about 200 birds (up from about 25 in 1945). With the onset of the third millennium of this era, conservationists will begin establishing an additional migratory flock of whooping cranes, one that will breed on the prairie provinces of Canada and winter in the southeastern United States. Toward developing techniques to meet this goal, motorized migrations with sandhill cranes as research surrogates were conducted each year beginning in 1995. In some experiments, sandhill cranes were led south by ultralight aircraft. In the two experiments described here, cranes were led south behind a truck.

The history of whooping crane conservation is so important to this story that later in the book (Chapter 5), I interrupt the narrative and supply historical details as a terse scientific monologue. Why? First, because it fits; second, because my publisher asked me to do it; and third, because it was not difficult to create: I merely updated and "popularized" the text of an earlier publication. Reader, if you don't want this tedious background information, just skip Chapter 5.

Before proceeding, I will also introduce the human players and express my thanks to them and a few others. For the first year (1995), four besides me participated in the training in Arizona. In 1996 our team included six people. Another, larger group helped rear chicks each year in Maryland before they were shipped to Arizona: Trish Fontaine was the most important player in rearing the 1996 flock. Sue Thomas spent much time rearing chicks and training them to walk the ramp during the pilot year, 1994, when we did not migrate birds. The team leader in both years of the migration was Brian Clauss, a Maryland native and an aviculturist at Patuxent. Two other key players who attended both years were R. Curt Mykut, also from Maryland, who proved to be cool-headed and capable at the wheel and elsewhere and Tsuyoshi (Yoshi) Watanabe, a graduate student from Hokaido, Japan. He used chicks in the 1995 cohort for his Master of Science research, but in 1996 joined us again just for the migration merely because he was anxious for our success. His contributions, repeatedly mentioned in the text, were profound. Matt Kinloch, another long time Maryland resident, helped rear chicks both years at Patuxent but came to Arizona only in 1995. He proved to be an able counselor, both for Brian and for me.

Three other young men joined the Arizona contingent in 1996. Dan Sprague from Maryland had worked at Patuxent for several years and brought to the project his experience in electronics. Matt Shawkey, an undergraduate from Connecticut and a volunteer at Patuxent, proved a valued helper on all phases of the training and a willing extra hand during the migration. Some of his eccentricities added to the novelty of the 1996 expedition. Dan Mummert, a native of Pennsylvania and a recent baccalaureate recipient, showed up as a volunteer late in our 1996 training but proved valuable during the expedition south and even more important during the late fall releases with all the pandemonium that followed.

Another eccentric who participated during a portion of 1996 was Robert Doyle. Robert's tales of terror from New Guinea entertained us as much as his able help facilitated our work. Robert, an aviculturist at the Baltimore Zoo, was indirectly the one who decided the date of the onset of our 1996 trek south: he had an obligatory departure date, so I started the expedition sooner than I wanted to insure that he had an opportunity to participate in the actual migration to reward his selfless service during training.

I must also mention two other participants. Joseph Duff is a professional photographer and a major player with Bill Lishman in the Operation Migration ultralight migrations from Ontario. Joe spent a week, gratis, documenting the 1996 migration. He proved indefatigable and cheerful throughout. Finally, and far from least, I mention Ben Trahan, my friend for twenty-five years. He volunteered to take time from his salaried work to accompany both migrations. Ben is mentioned frequently in the text, so I will save the details for later.

It is imperative that I mention, Dr. George Gee, leader of the crane research and propagation program at Patuxent. Without his encouragement the project would have never fledged. Many people at Patuxent headquarters and at the International Crane Foundation, most notably Claire Mirande, offered ideas that helped shape the study. My thanks also go to Wayne Shifflet, manager of the Buenos Aires National Wildlife Refuge, who hosted our wintering cranes. Sally Gall, Pam Landin, and Guy Jontz assisted with bird care at the refuge. Farm owners, Roy Pierpoint, the Rayner brothers, Delmar John, and Gene (el pistelero) Nixon provided a semi-safe haven for our wintering cranes in 1996–1999.

We are greatly indebted to Col. Larry Triphahn for allowing our training on the Navajo Army Depot near Belmont, Arizona. Sergeant Don Hack coordinated all our activities on the depot and sponsored our stay. John G. Goodwin, Jr. helped coordinate the study as did Phil Smith. Both are biologists with the Arizona Game and Fish

Department. Heather Greene, biologist with the Mormon Lake District of the Coconino National Forest, helped coordinate our many visits to Mormon Lake. Further, Heather and her associate, Lorie Shaull, often checked on our birds from the bluff overlooking the lake. My friend, Chuck LaRue, perhaps the most astute wildlife observer I have ever known, regularly drove the twenty miles from Flagstaff to check on our birds at Mormon Lake. I thank Billi Wagner for her lovely little crane drawings that fill in the empty spaces in the text.

Patrick Coronado, Charles Hoisington, and Jon Robinson, all at the NASA facility at the Goddard Space Flight Center in Greenbelt, Maryland, coordinated and financed much of the satellite telemetry aspects of our efforts. Without satellite telemetry many of the peregrinations of our long-legged charges would have remained a mystery.

Finally, I thank my wife, Cathy, for her many contributions. She acted as point-of-contact for both migrations, filled in as assistant crane handler, word processed and reviewed this book and the associated scientific publications, hosted the many craniac visits, and ferried gear and personnel. She did this and more without hope of monetary reward. Without her help, this book would be either far inferior or not at all.

Some apologies are also in order: to Martha Duck (a resident of the Antelope Hills Golf Course), to operators of the Casa Grande Golf Course, to guards and inmates of the state penitentiary at Florence, Arizona, and to a host of others (some named in the text) who were at first dazzled and later inconvenienced by our too-tame cranes. In addition I wish to thank Dan Mazullo, Jovita Fine, and others at the Heritage Park Zoo, Prescott, Arizona for holding our 1995 survivors in juvenile detention for part of the winter of 1996–1997. Christy Van Cleave, Arizona's number one raptor rehabilitator, collected and cared for some of our delinquent and injured birds on several occasions and even shared her bedroom for weeks with a special crane. Finally, Val Little and the Nature Conservancy staff at the Hassayampa River Reserve have my thanks for harboring Dennis, our most delinquent crane, through the winter of 1995–1996.

Again I offer my thanks and my apologies to all who bore the brunt of unrequested adventures and unrelenting inconveniences. I remain, however, fully aware that neither condolences nor coin are necessary or sufficient to return any of you to what you were before these stentorian creatures entered your lives.

Chapter 1

The Pioneers

T raining birds to follow humans is far from new: for more than 5,000 years, falconers around the world have trained raptors. Very often this resulted in the bird following a pedestrian or equestrian falconer for distances up to a few kilometers. More often, however, the falconer followed the bird as it pursued its quarry or sought its fancy elsewhere: who was the trainer and who the trainee? Marco Polo gave us a glimpse of the magnitude of falconry in 13th century China. He reported that when Hooblai Han (pronounced Who-bl-eye Hawn, popularly known in the West as Kublai Khan) went hawking, he was "attended by fully 10,000 falconers. . . ." Some falconers in such parties hunted cranes with gyrfalcons and even wolves with the byerkoot (golden eagle).

By the 1970s, raptor enthusiasts had trained several species of birds of prey to follow automobiles. In the 1980s, two remarkable experiments were conducted by Kenneth Franklin in Washington state. First, he trained two prairie falcons to circle up, join an ultralight aircraft, and then pursue it for food. Later, he trained peregrine falcons to follow him in free fall as he and the falcon sky dived from a small fixed-wing aircraft. Less spectacular, but more pertinent to our crane experiments, in 1979 and 1980 John McNeely trained a red-tailed hawk to fly with his hang glider. The bird often lit on the craft and received food from John as he flew. An award-winning mini-movie, "John McNeely and the Hawk," resulted from this experiment.

By the middle decades of the 20th century, scientists had a good understanding of the "following response" for some species of birds and had trained neonatal waterfowl to follow humans. Also pertinent are the waterfowl training experiments of William H. Carrick who, over many years (1970–present), trained geese and swans to follow boats and other craft. This pioneering work led to the spectacular successes of Bill Lishman and Joe Duff in leading Canada geese on migration in 1993, 1994, and 1995 from Ontario to Virginia and later to South Carolina.

Probably all aviculturists who have reared cranes have noted the propensity of chicks to follow their human caretakers. Beginning in 1973, George Archibald, co-founder and director of the International Crane Foundation in Baraboo, Wisconsin, trained sandhill cranes to rise up into the sky, then return to him. He added Eurasian cranes in 1975 until he had a group of up to twenty cranes that would launch, climb to 100 m, fly for five minutes or so, and then return to him.

Des and Jen Bartlett were probably the first to lead a crane chick with a motorized vehicle. In 1971, they reared a sandhill crane chick with a flock of snow geese and trained all the birds to follow an automobile. Because their goal was primarily to photograph the birds in flight, they made no attempt to actually lead the birds along a migration route with the vehicle. They did, however, periodically release the crane and geese at refuges scattered along their route from southern Canada to Texas.

Beginning in 1983, Idaho wheat farmer and *de facto* biologist, Kent Clegg, led tame sandhill cranes behind "all terrain" vehicles and automobiles. In 1994, one such flight extended to 38 miles behind a pickup truck. Kent Clegg in the West, and Joe Duff and Bill Lishman in the East, later each led their own crane migrations using ultralight aircraft.

Each year from 1990 through 1992, we at Patuxent trained four to six sandhill crane chicks to follow a motor vehicle. Our goal was to observe the flight performance of the cranes while they wore various harnesses carrying satellite transmitters. We wanted to make sure that attaching a satellite backpack (to give us important migration data) would not endanger the life of wild cranes while they traveled south. Because much of Patuxent is forested, these flights never exceeded half a mile.

These independent and usually unpublicized experiments bring us to 1993 when it was decided by the Canadian and U.S. Whooping Crane Recovery Teams that a method should be developed to lead cranes south from a reintroduction site not then chosen in southern Canada. Ultimately, the preferred method should teach the cranes a specific migration pathway that they would faithfully use year after year.

Chapter 2

Preparations

Only four minutes late, Dr. George Gee, leader of the crane research program at Patuxent, entered, took a chair, then informally but courteously announced, "I guess we had better get started." Six scientists and two interested onlookers (including Brian Clauss, my deputy on the project) sat around a very long table in the dormer-like conference room in the Merriam Laboratory at the Patuxent Wildlife Research Center, Maryland. George spoke, and six scientists interrupted their cheerful babblings to focus on one project. Their mission was to decide if the proposed motorized migrations had enough scientific merit to deserve endorsement by the group and funding by Patuxent, by the Department of the Interior, by the U.S. Congress, and by the American people.

I had my own doubts about the project. This was arguably the most bizarre scientific experiment I had ever even heard about, let alone proposed as my own. With only a perfunctory introduction, George called on me to explain the project. I cleared my throat, blanched, and realized that everyone in the room had already read the study plan, had the same doubts I had, and had generated a few doubts of their own. I long ago learned a valuable lesson: the fastest way to defuse an argument is to say what your opponent is thinking. I opened, "Basically, we have no idea what we're doing." Having so said, I sat there trying to look vulnerable, but deep-down inside I was thinking, "Touché. No one in this room is going to offer a criticism more penetrating than my own."

After my expression of ignorance, Brian, who unfortunately for himself shares my same warped sense of humor, muffled his laughter and looked around trying to see who might be offended by his levity. After the ice was broken, we just settled into a free exchange of ideas. Someone thought we should make the sidewalls of a truck transparent so the cranes could see out while riding south. Dr. Matt Perry suggested we obviate the lengthy and expensive process of training cranes and merely build a plexiglass box, then fly the birds south suspended below a helicopter. No one laughed. How could it be that no one laughed? The idea was absolutely ridiculous. How could anyone not laugh? Then I remembered . . . my proposal was to make the birds fly south behind a truck.

Actually, my opening statement was inaccurate. In fact, we knew a great deal about what we were doing and how to do it. We had trained cranes for three years to follow a truck over short distances, and in 1994 we had trained five crane chicks to walk a ramp into and out of a truck. We also had transported them at high speeds while they rode in the net-covered truck bed. Yes, in retrospect, we knew very well what we were doing, but my expression of ignorance made it a lot easier for the scientists to offer ideas in a realm far from their personal experience and to approve a project that was more than a little odd. And approval did come.

During our pilot study in 1994, we found it a little difficult to train cranes to walk a ramp. To do so, we scattered mealworms on the ground, up the long ramp, and into the truck bed. It also helped, in coaxing the chicks along, to imitate appropriate crane calls and to toss food.

Ramp training began when the chicks were about ten days old. All chicks quickly learned to walk up the ramp and down. A minor difficulty was in preventing the flightless chicks from walking off the edge of the ramp. Wild sandhill cranes do not land in trees, so they do not possess a behavioral mechanism to prevent walking over edges. It became necessary to station a caretaker on each side of the ramp, otherwise we would have had chicks with broken legs.

In 1994, none of the birds were trained to fly behind the truck, but we did have them ride in the truck after they were about 65 days old.

They showed very little aversion to riding in the bed of the truck, but when we sped to 60+ mph, the cranes instinctively lined up in the middle of the truck bed, behind the cab, and each kept its bill pointing forward lest it whip backwards over its shoulder in the fast-moving airstream.

Also in 1994, we began to search for a suitable migration corridor for a long-distance trucking study. Our goal was to find a northern terminus with good habitat for sandhill cranes but where sandhill cranes no longer breed. We reasoned that, for the sandhill crane study to best approximate the conditions in the future whooping crane migration projects, it was important for the sandhill crane chicks to not have wild sandhill cranes available to lead our birds on migration, either north or south. It was our goal to find a route removed from any currently used sandhill crane migration corridor.

In my quest for a route, I looked first at northern termini in Maine, New York, and Ontario with routes south to Atlantic coastal marshes. In my mind's eye, I envisioned my birds winging their way south between the twin towers of the World Trade Center. To arrange any route, permission must be obtained from each state. When I informally discussed an Atlantic coast route with the Atlantic Flyway Council, the group that mediates waterfowl hunting and related topics for the region, their response, as worded by Jerry Serie, questioned my sanity. "Why would you want to try such an obviously hazardous thing along the most heavily populated corridor in North America?" I had visited each state along various Atlantic seaboard routes and had secretly been wondering the same thing myself. I turned west.

It would be an additional benefit if our experiment would result in the reestablishment of the sandhill crane as a breeding bird in some high, cold marsh in the Colorado Rockies, but to do the work in Colorado would result in our birds, while on migration, joining other flocks of sandhill cranes on their way south to New Mexico for the winter. After months of staring at maps and fretting, we settled on a route leading south from the mountains of northern Arizona to the Buenos Aires National Wildlife Refuge on the Mexican border. If we used this route, the northern terminus was ideal because sandhill cranes had formerly bred there, at least until 1886, but sandhill cranes were now absent as breeders and unlikely even as migrants. The Buenos Aires NWR was chosen as the winter terminus because sandhill cranes never winter there, seldom migrate past, and because facilities were available to overwinter the birds in a pen safe from predation. We had no interest in determining coyote predation rates on tame cranes living in a marshless desert.

So Arizona was chosen. On advice from John G. Goodwin, Jr., a research biologist with the Arizona Game and Fish Department and a longtime friend, we began working with the Arizona National Guard to decide if their base, known as Camp Navajo, a dozen miles west of Flagstaff, would be a suitable place to camp for a month or so and train our cranes to fly with the truck. By early 1994, I had opened correspondence with Sergeant Don Hack, and in November 1994, I visited the site and tried to convince the base commander and his staff that the sandhill crane was not endangered and that we had no clandestine plan to introduce endangered whooping cranes and thereby shut down the base. In America today, the only thing more frightening than losing another endangered species is discovering that an endangered species lives in your backyard, can't tolerate lawn mowers, and is allergic to barbeque smoke. Once permission was granted, we settled on Camp Navajo.

Sandhill crane cowering, a submissive posture.

Chapter 3

The Route South

C amp Navajo looked ideal as a training site. During late summer I began searching for the exact route south. The quickest way to go by car from Camp Navajo to the Buenos Aires NWR is to follow the divided interstate highway east to Flagstaff, then south to Phoenix and Tucson. These highways are posted at 75 mph and are often driven much faster. Cranes fly at 30-35 mph. Even when flying downhill, 45 is the normal maximum flight speed. Not wanting to explain to the police why we were driving 30 in a zone posted 75 mph, we chose back roads.

I spent much of August and September staring at Arizona state maps, wetland maps, county maps, Army Map Service maps, and Forest Service maps. Several alternate routes were chosen, then I climbed into my vintage International Scout and began the tedious task of deciding which dirt roads could be driven at 30 mph minimum (so the cranes wouldn't get confused, pass the truck, then pick their own route). My goal was to find as direct a route as practical without long east-west legs and no north legs to confuse the cranes when in future years they would traverse the route alone.

I finally settled on a 387-mile-long, S-shaped route through fairly open habitat (once we left the ponderosa pine forests at the north end). From Camp Navajo, we would wind southwest down off the Mogollon Rim, into Chino Valley, around the Bradshaw Mountains, over the Weaver Mountains, then southeast to Picacho Reservoir, and finally south to the Buenos Aires NWR on the Mexican border. In choosing roads, it appeared I would have to abandon my first rule and take the birds twenty miles west before I could turn south, but by early September, I found a Forest Service road that came only four miles from our training area on Camp Navajo. It jogged south, then west, then southwest, and lined up with a little-used paved road leading southwest into Chino Valley. Then we would cross Hell Canyon and continue southwest around Sullivan Buttes and into Skull Valley. The roads were all there on the map, but could I gain access to those that crossed private property?

In Skull Valley, we also needed a place to camp. Some two miles south of the village, I spotted an irrigated meadow that looked inviting for cranes. It also had long lines of towering cottonwood trees that would shade the crane caretakers. I drove in to inquire. There weren't many alternate places and none so good as this, so I was nervous about my approach. Two faded-muzzle mongrels growled menacingly as I stepped out of the car. At times like this, you can't just throw a rock at someone else's dog. But dogs are very smart and a slight feint as if reaching for a stone will most of the time make all but the most vicious canines give ground.

I thumped at the door of the screen porch. A few moments later, a tall, slim, white-mustached cowhand emerged without his hat. Time and sun had left his cranial dome bleached even more than the grizzled canines that paced menacingly at my rear. He looked like a range rider not a ranch owner, but his stately bearing confused me, so I launched into a lengthy description of my mission and the cranes that would

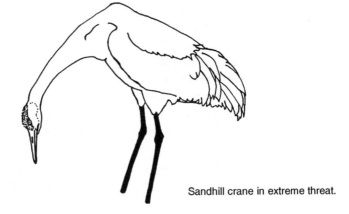

Sandhill crane in extreme threat.

18

wing their way south this October. Then I blurted out my request for a place to camp with my birds.

Some of you, from your own experiences, can sympathize with me. Have you ever, after a lengthy explanation, discovered you are talking to the wrong department? Well, this fellow looked me over and noted that I was traveling with neither a black hat, spurs, oversized belt buckle, nor pointed-toed boots. He sized me up for a city slicker, then expressed his opinion that he didn't think much of the project and figured the meadow was intended for cows. Fortunately, he was not the rightful owner.

Dave Jenner, the real owner, would elude my visits for another three weeks. Finally, I decided to just call him on the phone. Now, if you understand telemarketing, you know that a phone request is the easiest to dismiss, so I did not have high hopes when I called. I tried to remember my teenage Colorado cowboy accent and to de-emphasize that this was a federal government project involving young guys from Maryland (long hair and maybe an earring or two), but all of this concern was probably for naught. As it turned out, Dave Jenner was an aged, kindly man, anxious to help. Yes, we could rest our birds, and if we wanted to camp, no problem.

Not all my negotiations went so well. A broad, antelope-browsed grassland extends around the north end of Sullivan Buttes. Big Chino Road leads to the Sullivan Buttes, and five miles to the west, another high speed dirt road leads south into Skull Valley. That five miles belongs to a Mr. John Punchcow. To go around Mr. Punchcow's five miles of grassland would require a 40-mile circuitous detour around the Sullivan Buttes. Everything else had been arranged, from Camp Navajo to the Mexican border. A locked gate guarded the grassland, and John Punchcow figuratively guarded the gate. Unfortunately, John Punchcow didn't attend Sunday School with Dave Jenner.

The first neighbor I asked knew exactly who owned the lock on the gate and thought it not worth my time to try to arrange permission. The person who said, "It never hurts to ask," hadn't met John Punchcow. From the signs along the fences, it looked like you could get shot asking permission, so I telephoned. A son answered, and said his dad was hospitalized after a rodeo accident. No, the son wasn't going to the hospital, and he did not think it would work if Mrs. Punchcow asked her husband in the hospital. A week later, I caught Mrs. Punchcow on the phone. She said it was a bad idea even to ask.

Being naturally pugnacious myself, I was sort of looking forward to speaking with this guy. Another week went by, I called, and Mr. Punchcow was finally home. When he picked up the phone, I stammered out the purpose of my call, then waxed eloquent: what a wondrous thing it would be if sandhill cranes once again bred in Arizona; how grand it would be if they migrated past his ranch; and perhaps the technique he helped us develop could be used to enable the whooping crane to once again grace the marshes and prairies of Manitoba. As I droned on, I was starting to wonder if John Punchcow had already hung up. Finally, Mr. Punchcow interrupted my monologue. No, he didn't have any interest in the project and wouldn't help. End of conversation.

We shifted to Plan B: fly the birds to the Punchcow gate at the east side of Sullivan Buttes, truck them forty miles to the Punchcow sign, "Warning: No Trespassing, No Hunting, No Woodcutting," on the west side of Sullivan Buttes, then free the birds to fly south.

As the end of September approached, every other obstacle had been cleared. We had our route picked out. None of it was on divided highways, and only a little of it was on roads too bumpy for wild men to drive at 35 mph. There were, however, more than a hundred and twenty sets of powerlines waiting to filter our birds out of the sky.

Sandhill crane ready to attack.

Chapter 4

Rearing and Training the Cranes

O ne other preparation was necessary to make our project work. We needed a truck big enough to haul our little flock. That spring, our veterinarians at Patuxent had been wrangling support for a mobile hospital. They found a nice, used ambulance for a third of the cost of a new one. They also found an army ambulance (MASH wagon) they could get free from Ft. George Meade (of Civil War fame) just across the Patuxent River from our headquarters. Now the vets wanted the nifty white used ambulance, and I wanted the MASH wagon. They lacked money and permission to buy used (government rules), so I got involved, offered to lend some of my satellite telemetry money and help arrange permission for them to buy the used vehicle. The result was that with lots of encouragement from me, but very little effort and no money on my part, they got their ambulance and I got the MASH truck, free.

The eight-foot cots came out. One became the crane ramp. A weekend and a few evenings later, we had a hinged floor with rubber mats, a plexiglass forward wall, a plexiglass door to the driver's compartment, and carpet on the firewall (so we could think while the engine was running). All the beast needed now was a name. It, by consensus, became "the cranemobile." The cranemobile was further distinguished by golden auto customizing strips on the roof and doors, and a full-sized, white crane silhouette painted on the roof.

Crane chicks have been reared at the Patuxent Wildlife Research Center since 1966. The Center is home not only to the world's largest captive crane colony with more than 300 birds each fall (before the young birds are sent out for release), but Patuxent also houses the Bird Banding Laboratory where banding records are stored for all migratory birds banded in the United States and Canada. Globally important teams also conduct research on pesticides, other pollutants, and on the population ecology of endangered or migratory species.

In late May, Brian Clauss and his crew at Patuxent, got the first news that hatching of the greater sandhill crane chicks was imminent. They had known for weeks that the eggs were fertile and viable. Much like a human child can be felt punching and kicking within its mother's womb months before birth, crane embryos also kick and lurch within the egg. All you have to do is place the egg in a liquid bath and wait for movement. We use warm water laced with betadine, an antibiotic, to float our eggs. If a late-term chick is alive, the floating egg will bob and lurch: it's the chick's way of saying all is well.

Three days prior to hatching, the crane chicks break into the air cell at the large end of the egg. At once they begin pulmonary respiration, and, now that they are breathing, they also begin to chirp and whistle from within the still unpipped shell. Once they begin to call, we reciprocate. It is late May and even though I am chasing eagles in Mongolia, the chicks have to spend fifteen minutes, every three hours, each day listening to a tape recording of my imitation of the brood call of a sandhill crane parent. They listen not only to my brood call, but also to a recording of cranemobile engine noises and two flags popping in the wind. These flags will one day top the cranemobile as it treks across Arizona leading our sandhills south. To make sure our chicks will know they are cranes, we rear them next door to a live adult crane imprinting model. When tiny, each gets a stuffed crane head feeder model and a stuffed whole crane brooder model with a heat lamp overhead.

The first year of the study (1995), we did not disguise ourselves in the ghost costumes used for about fifteen years by most crane reintroduction teams so their cranes would not be tame toward uncostumed humans after release. I opted to not force my crane-rearing team to spend much of the humid Maryland summer draped in gray from crown to toe. Once we were certain we could get the cranes to follow the cranemobile long distances (this happened in the 1995 migration), I reconsidered. So, in 1996, we all spent more than enough time dressed as ghosts. In 1995, we distinguished ourselves from the general public by wearing a special anorak and a red baseball cap.

During transport in a vehicle, the long-legged cranes were, of course, thrown off balance by every bump and turn. For three decades, I have been accompanied by some sort of hawk, eagle, or owl on many of my expeditions, so I have long since learned to round out the corners and compensate for bumps. Cranes are very tall, so problems caused by changes in momentum are aggravated. However, all of our crew members quickly learned to accelerate and decelerate slowly so our cranes could be transported moderate distances with little discomfort.

When loading small chicks into the truck, we used a one-foot tall fence along both sides of the ramp. After the chicks were about thirty days old, the ramp fence was neither tall enough nor necessary, but even after the ramp was removed, trainers continued to protect the chicks as they climbed the ramp.

Even from the beginning, each chick had its own unique personality. As with human children, sometimes the wildest neophytes settle down nicely long before their adolescence. Not so Baka. Although far from the oldest, whenever she was taken out of her private pen and placed with her training cohort, Baka would rage about, attacking even the tallest chicks. Sometimes the big males would stab back before giving ground, but eventually even the biggest adolescent gave way to the tippy-toe assaults of this pint-sized ruffian.

It looked like Baka would have to stay in Maryland: neither the other colts nor the caretakers could control this gruine hellion. Then, overnight, she changed. Brian and I decided it was time for a trial run before our 2,300 mile drive transporting the colts from Maryland to Arizona, so on 8 August, he and Matt loaded Baka and one other chick into the cranemobile, headed for Annapolis, crossed the Chesapeake Bay Bridge, and then on to the Clauss family farm near Pokomoke City. Bouncing around in the truck and camping out overnight made the difference. Baka transformed into one of our most cooperative birds.

From this experience, we developed a technique called abandonment training. This is how you do it. Transport the errant bird to a remote location just as is normally done with a group of flockmates. Next, conceal a caretaker, then load all the cranes except the delinquent

23

trainee into the cranemobile. At first the trainee is relieved to be free of his nuisance companions, but very soon he realizes that he is lost, they aren't coming back, and even his costumed mother is absent. Anxiety turns to panic. After an hour or so of this, the caretaker emerges, "finds" the crane and behold, the prodigal has been reformed. Although I have never tried it, I am quite certain this technique will also work to make your kids "grocery store safe."

All aspects of training, except flying behind the truck, were initiated prior to transporting the birds west. Because of our decades-long experiences with leg and wing injuries in newly-fledged chicks at Patuxent, we decided to wait to transport the birds to Arizona until the youngest bird was more than seventy days of age. The long bones of sandhill cranes are fully grown by this age and the birds are less susceptible to injury during travel.

The crane colts we chose were transported to Arizona in two ways. The four oldest were loaded into the cranemobile on 24 August and the craniacs headed west. The other cranes were to be crated and flown in after the craniacs arrived in Arizona. Once I knew the cranes and keepers were on the road, I began preparations for their arrival. First, I assembled the tents and other gear they would need plus a huge square net to serve as a crane pen. As they progressed across the country, they called periodically so I could estimate the time of their arrival. With some time to spare, I headed for the Navajo Army Depot from my home in southern Arizona and arrived at the cranes' proposed summer home, an open, grasshopper-buzzing meadow near two small ponds, all of which was surrounded by a dense stand of stately ponderosa pines. Prior to their arrival, I constructed a pen in an open area between several small ponderosa pines. My plan was that the cranes would stay there, close to the open prairie while the craniacs could camp in separate two-man tents in the shade of the nearby pines. A family-sized tent would serve as a storage area. I wanted the craniacs to choose their own sites for their tents and gear, but I rushed to have the net up and ready for the cranes as soon as they arrived. I suspended a white nylon rope between five pines, then dropped the net over it and rewove the rope under the net and around the trees. Decades earlier, I had gained considerable experience "hanging seine" while working as a deck hand on salmon boats in the Gulf of Alaska. That experience was called into use as I worked furiously to attach the net to each tree, weave in a door,

24

and secure the net to the ground with boulders. I was much relieved to finish before my crew arrived.

At 3 p.m. on 27 August, the cranemobile bumped down the dusty Army road toward me. They arrived only two hours later than projected. What could I expect? No one had ever trucked cranes thousands of miles cross country before. It was hard to determine who looked more bedraggled, the cranes or the craniacs. All of the birds were weak and wobbly. Our biggest male, 86, had spent most of the last two days slumped in sitting posture, wings drooped on the deck. From his appearance upon arrival, I expected him to die.

After the three other cranes were safely down, Curt climbed into the cranemobile and straddled 86's fallen body. Gently he helped him to his feet. Stimulated by the unwanted attention, 86 rallied and actually leapt out of the cranemobile to the ground. He then spread his wings for balance and stumbled along. I expected him to collapse, but instead he lurched forward, spread his wings, and actually lifted off. We stood amazed as he flapped along, but after only a hundred feet or so, he touched down and crumpled into a disheveled heap. He sat there in a daze, bill tip nearly touching the ground.

Within two days, all but 86 were well-coordinated, active, and had begun flight training. Gradually, 86 commenced flight training, although it was not until nine days after arrival that he participated fully with the other cranes. The evidence of their ordeal was written in the plumage of all four birds. After their feathers had grown out completely, each one showed a broad, weak, and imperfectly formed band that corresponded with their journey west and evidenced the heavy stress of that trek.

Our six remaining cranes were flown from Maryland to Flagstaff on 28 August in a small jet, a Cessna Citation. These birds spent only eight hours in special shipping crates, wooden boxes tall enough for them to stand. None of these birds showed damage during shipment other than temporarily mussed bustles. All were alert and ready to begin training upon arrival. I greatly appreciate Terry Kohler, of water fixture fame, for transporting these six cranes, gratis.

Flight training began on 30 August. Each morning, the rear doors of the cranemobile were locked open and one or more of the craniacs climbed onto the elevated truck bed. Another craniac pegged the net gate open and herded the birds quickly out of their pen. Excitedly peeping, they strode toward the waiting crew. When the intensity reached its zenith, the driver and all hands began loudly trilling, "G-g-g-g-g-g-wowww," and waving to the birds. The cranes leaned forward showing their flight intention posture. The cranemobile lurched forward, accelerating as rapidly as possible, trying to stay ahead of the cranes as they ran, flapped, and finally lifted off.

Further stimulation was provided by two flags affixed above roof level. Our decision to use flags was fortuitous. Even through our truck engine was very loud, we could hear the flags popping in the wind, and more importantly, the cranes could hear the flags even when they could not see the truck as it wound through the forest below them.

Our early flights began near camp. As the cranemobile lumbered forward with our little flock in rapid pursuit, it arrived at the first turn, a sharp left. The birds swung past to the right, then quickly made the correction and were hot on the cranemobile's tail when it entered the woods. Next came two minutes of swaying left and right as the truck rushed (too fast for safety) around each corner, through the chuck holes, over the boulders, and on through the woods.

It rather amazed me just how efficiently our team worked. Each week I came to visit my young friends, check on the crane's progress, and participate in one or two training sessions before departing to explore our future route south. With Brian inconspicuously at the helm, the guys divided up the camp chores, tested the telemetry equipment, moved pens, and conducted the training sessions, all with never an angry word. They seemed a perfect team. The task one craniac hated, someone else preferred. Through time, this division of labor, though never openly stated, became the norm. Brian, having survived an automobile rollover, preferred riding in the dusty back of the cranemobile watching the cranes and trying not to think about the hazards ahead. Yoshi was probably the most influential in deciding the timbre around camp. Thoroughly Japanese, he could never get over bowing, hands open and at thigh level, whenever he greeted us. So we all learned to bow and say, "Good morning," and "Oh, thank you." Americanoid grunts and scoffs were decidedly out of style in this camp.

No one should think this admission any sort of indictment that my crew was stiff, pious, or stuffy. Not so. Brian, for example, was heavily sarcastic elsewhere, but for our project, he and everyone else worked hard to be friendly, cheerful, and courteous, everything Boy Scouts pledge to be but sometimes aren't. So what were the specific niches for Matt, Yoshi, and Curt? Matt and Curt were the experienced drivers. Yoshi was so careful and courteous behind the wheel of his own car that he had zero experience at the roughneck driving necessary to keep the cranemobile right side up and ahead of the cranes. After Yoshi tipped the cranemobile onto only two wheels during one training flight, I decided to capitalize instead on his excellent abilities to gather and organize data. Because of his diligence in this role, we have accurate data for every training flight, the identity of each crane in each flight, how far they flew, how high they flew, and how fast. Other minutia, so painful to record, but so necessary in scientific reporting, also fell to Yoshi. Brian, by contrast, although recognizing the need for paperwork, was more than happy for Yoshi to be the recorder.

Curt was the most experienced outdoors man, so it fell to him to advise the others on camp matters. He also had considerable four-wheel-drive experience, and I was always more comfortable when either he or I was at the wheel of the cranemobile, our only non-expendable vehicle. Matt was good at everything, but proved to be a right-hand man and "idea person" for Brian. Every person on our crew contributed good ideas, but I think Matt was best. Weekly, he would generate novel approaches, volunteer these in a disinterested fashion, and support the project even if his "better way" was not adopted.

As an aside, I should describe a humorous anecdote involving Matt. When he left Maryland, it was so hot that he needed an air conditioner to sleep comfortably, so Matt was surprised and unprepared for the almost nightly freezes at 7,000 feet. Knowing of his nocturnal battles with hypothermia, I surprised him with an army surplus, down sleeping bag (probably World War II vintage) with lots of leaks. Thereafter, Matt emerged each morning warm, but with a generous coating of feathers, evidence of his nightly efforts to keep the duck from escaping.

At the onset, flights were short (one to two miles), but by the end of September, the birds were making ten-mile flights followed by about a ten minute rest, then a return flight of up to ten miles. The birds were flown through the development on base, across the prairie areas, and through the forest patches, all in preparation for the hazards and distractions of the migration pathway.

27

Our birds also needed training to avoid flying into fences and powerlines. We began by stopping our initial flights immediately after going under a powerline. This way the birds were going very slowly when they encountered the line and were unlikely to hurt themselves if they bumped into it. To introduce the hazards of fences, the guys built a thirty-foot section of fence right by camp. It temporarily and incompletely served to keep the birds out of camp, but more importantly, it taught them that pacing a fence does no good: you have to go around.

By late September, the birds had flown fifty-three flights on twenty-three days over a thirty-four-day period. They flew a total of 140 miles with a total flight time of five hours and one minute. The average altitude was sixty feet with the highest being about 200 feet. They averaged 29 mph, but flew as fast as 45 mph and as slow as 15 mph. Thanks to Yoshi, I can report these values with some certainty.

These flights were always exciting: each one was unique and, at least in retrospect, humorous. Once when bouncing along in the cranemobile with the cranes in hot pursuit, we swept past three camo-clad bow hunters. They just stood there, slack-jawed, watching as we lumbered past, squawking and flapping and billowing dust. Slowly the question formed, "Why? Why are four guys with red baseball caps, flapping arms and squawking like big chickens?" The answer washed over them like a summer storm. Ten cranes swept in from behind, barely overhead, in hot pursuit of the truck. Three well-camouflaged hunters looked up, jaws even slacker. "Why are the big birds chasing the truck?"

Because we hoped that our cranes would eventually breed in the marshes where sandhill cranes had bred a century earlier, on 13 September we trucked them to Mormon Lake and allowed them to wander in the marshes. We also encouraged them to capture grasshoppers and aquatic insects in the marshes at Camp Navajo. Matt bought a minnow net, and the crew spent an hour or so each day wading around with the birds, encouraging them to eat snails, fish, frogs, and aquatic insects. Even more time was spent wandering the prairie catching grasshoppers and crickets.

And so the summer passed. Each day our flock was a little closer to the time when the real hazards would come. No one had ever led cranes on migration before . . . would it work?

Chapter 5

The First Half of the Whooping Crane Comeback Story

Of the fifteen species of cranes worldwide, six are legally decreed to be endangered. All fifteen species have been bred in captivity, and during the last twenty years, great progress has been made in developing propagation and reintroduction techniques that, it is hoped, will assist in the recovery of the whooping crane. This book is about some of these efforts. The training migrations were conducted with the sandhill crane, the most populous crane in the world. The sandhill crane does not need our help, but it is a good research surrogate for the whooping crane. The account of whooping crane conservation that follows is an update of a scientific paper I published several years ago.

Robert Porter Allen, who studied the whooping crane for many years, mapped out what he believed to be the historical breeding range of the whooping crane. This area extended from Illinois northwest through Iowa, Minnesota, and North Dakota into southern Manitoba, Saskatchewan, and Alberta. A disjunct population nested in the Great Slave Lake region. In 1939, a small, nonmigratory population was found breeding in the marshes north of White Lake, Louisiana. Breeding may have also occurred at other locations, but information is insufficient. Wintering populations ranged from the Rio Grande delta, eastward along the Gulf Coast to Florida and northward along the Atlantic Coast as far as New Jersey. In the 1800s, a combination of habitat destruction, human disturbance, hunting, and egg and specimen collection for museums and private collectors contributed to a rapid

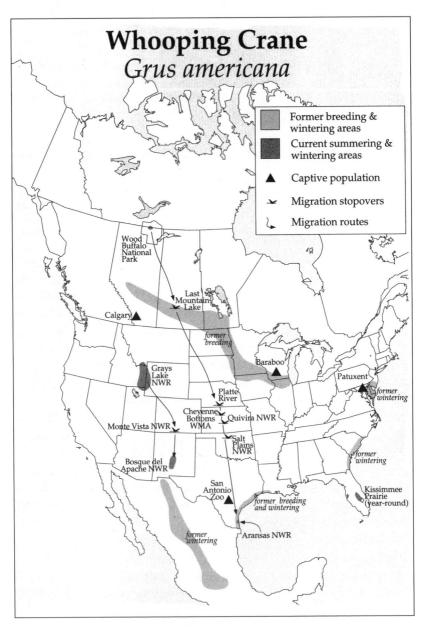

Fig. 1 Distribution of the Whooping Crane
Map by Milford Muskett

population decline. By 1870, fewer than 1,400 individuals remained. In 1945, the population consisted of two disjunct flocks totaling about twenty-one birds, with only three birds remaining of the small, soon to be extinct, sedentary flock in Louisiana. The other eighteen birds comprised a flock that wintered at Aransas, along the Texas Gulf Coast and nested in Wood Buffalo National Park, Northwest Territories, Canada. Following this population nadir, the whooping crane began slowly to increase.

The ponderous but inexorable expansion of the whooping crane population beginning in the late 1940s prompted a search for management schemes to bolster the wild population. Captive breeding was attempted for many years with the few birds at Audubon Park Zoo in New Orleans (1948–1966), in confinement at Aransas (1948–1951), and at the San Antonio Zoo (1967 to present). The notion of establishing a sizable captive flock by removing young whooping cranes from the Aransas-Wood Buffalo population was first proposed by John Lynch in 1956. Theoretically, whooping cranes produced by the captive flock could then be released to augment the wild population and the captive flock could serve as a hedge against catastrophic loss. In 1957, Dayton Hyde noted that because sandhill cranes and whooping cranes usually lay two eggs but rarely raise two young, a captive flock could be established without detriment to the wild population by removing one egg from each clutch. Ray C. Erickson in 1968 recommended practicing the technique first by developing a surrogate flock of nonendangered sandhill cranes. In 1961, the U.S. Fish and Wildlife Service established a captive flock of sandhill cranes at Monte Vista National Wildlife Refuge in Colorado to develop crane husbandry and propagation techniques. In 1966, the surrogate flock and a flightless male whooping crane recovered in Canada in 1964 were moved to Patuxent. In 1967, the second eggs from six nests in Wood Buffalo were taken to Patuxent. Egg taking has continued sporadically almost until the present, with eggs sent either to Patuxent, to Grays Lake, Idaho, or, more recently, to the International Crane Foundation (ICF), Baraboo, Wisconsin. Management agencies and researchers generally believe that this egg harvest has not adversely affected (Ernie Kuyt suggested that it may have actually increased) the number of chicks fledged each fall in Canada. It sounds counterintuitive that an egg harvest would yield an increase, but two positive factors resulted from the harvest. First, when the harvest team visited the nests, they would float the eggs and if no eggs were viable in a particular nest, they would swap-in a viable egg collected elsewhere. Second, the survivability of a chick is probably increased by having it receive the additional parental attention that would have been shared with a brood mate if a second chick hatched.

During the colony's first decade at Patuxent, many disease and nutritional problems that initially impaired survival and breeding of whooping cranes in captivity were resolved. In 1975, the first fertile eggs were produced by a captive female at Patuxent. The first chick fledged in 1976. As problems with artificial insemination, incubation, and chick rearing were addressed, annual productivity increased. With these successes, it then became possible to address more subtle problems such as failure of neonatal young to feed, failure of pairs to bond and breed, and sexual imprinting of chicks on human caretakers.

Between 1975 and 1991, the Patuxent flock produced 255 eggs, of which seventy-three (sixty-one known to be fertile) were transferred in an attempt to establish a second wild flock at Grays Lake, Idaho. The captive population slowly expanded and a decision was made to establish a second captive breeding flock at a site remote from Patuxent. In November 1989, twenty-two birds representing all families in the captive flock were transferred to the International Crane Foundation in Baraboo, Wisconsin.

By 1947, only one wild bird remained in the marshes near White Lake, Louisiana (Fig. 1). In an effort to retain the genetic contribution of this bird, the crane was captured by helicopter on 11 March 1950 and translocated by truck to join the Aransas-Wood Buffalo flock. On arrival, the dangerously weakened crane was penned and force fed for two days, then released into a freshwater marsh where it was later attacked by two wild cranes. It was recaptured, fed, and released at a freshwater lake some distance from other whooping cranes. It survived through the spring and summer but was found dead in September. If nothing else, this attempt demonstrated some of the problems inherent in translocating adult cranes.

Long-term survival of whooping cranes can be ensured by establishing disjunct captive and wild populations. The U.S. and Canadian fish and wildlife services decided in 1986 that before the bird was "down listed" from endangered to threatened status, at least two additional wild flocks, each with a minimum of twenty-five nesting pairs must be established. "Delisting" would follow as even more flocks were established.

The first attempt at establishing another wild flock was a massive, long-term (1975–1988) effort. It consisted of placing 289 whooping crane eggs in greater sandhill crane nests at Grays Lake, Idaho. This experiment, led by Rod Drewien, was designed to create a disjunct population of whooping cranes that, like their sandhill crane foster parents, would nest in Idaho and winter along the Rio Grande River in west-central New Mexico.

According to the plan, the sandhill crane foster parents were to incubate the eggs and rear the young whooping cranes that hatched, and then lead the young whoopers on migration. However, Drewien reported that only 209 (72%) of the eggs transferred to Grays Lake hatched, and only 84 chicks (40% of the 209 that hatched or 29% of the original 289 eggs) fledged. High egg and chick mortality rates were associated with inclement weather, low water, and coyote predation. Most cranes that managed to fledge died from powerline and other wire strikes or from avian tuberculosis. The Grays Lake whooping crane flock declined from a high of 33 birds in 1984–1985 to 13 birds in 1991. Only three survived in 1997.

Abysmal survival of young birds at Grays Lake was followed by the failure of the few surviving whooping cranes to form pair bonds and breed. Among breeding-age birds, a preponderance of males caused by differences in male and female mortality contributed to this failure. More importantly, the few females that reached breeding age failed to pair with males on the wintering ground or at the spring staging areas. Rather, they scattered on northward migration, thereby further diminishing their chances of finding mates. Yearly attempts were made to capture these wandering females and transport them back to pair with wild males at Grays Lake but no pairing resulted. In the twenty-five years since the project began, only one offspring was produced, a hybrid between a whooper male and a sandhill female. In March 1990, a decision was made to de-emphasize the Grays Lake experiment.

Factors such as high mortality during migration (which may account for about 80% of the losses in the Aransas-Wood Buffalo flock), disease hazards, and demographics, all recommend that future reintroduction sites have all or some of the following characteristics:

33

(1) extensive suitable habitat, (2) geographical isolation from other wild populations (to limit effects of a single catastrophic mortality event such as an oil spill, storm, or epizootic), (3) a southern location that would discourage migration (and thereby limit migration-related mortality and negate the need to teach birds to migrate), and (4) a location within the historic range of the species. Using these criteria, an obvious choice for the next reintroduction of a sedentary population would be the marshes north of White Lake in southern Louisiana. It seems logical to return the birds to the wild where they most recently lived. The creation of a nonmigratory population is also preferred because of risks noted during migration in the Grays Lake experiment.

Until recently, White Lake appeared to be unavailable as a reintroduction site because state and federal wildlife management agencies had strong reservations. The state feared that the declaration of critical habitat would impair waterfowl hunting and other forms of wildlife use. Federal agents feared that local customs, especially wildlife harvesting practices, would endanger any released birds. As a consequence, three other sites were evaluated from 1984 to 1987: (1) the Upper Peninsula of Michigan, (2) Okefenokee Swamp in southern Georgia, and (3) the Kissimmee Prairie region in central Florida. All areas have extensive wetlands, are somewhat removed from urban areas, and currently support sizable sandhill crane populations. Whooping crane breeding, however, has never been documented for any of the three areas, although Allen reported evidence that the species occurred, and perhaps summered, in Florida even into the 20th century.

In 1988, the U.S. Fish and Wildlife Service decided to proceed with a whooping crane introduction experiment on the Kissimmee Prairie in Florida. Reasons favoring this area include the extent of wetland habitat, the potential for establishing a nonmigratory flock, the high degree of state and local support for the project, favorable land use practices, and favorable human demographics.

Releases began in 1993 under the leadership of Steve Nesbitt with about thirty cranes released each winter. By 1999, almost 180 young cranes had been freed. Unfortunately, bobcat predation was decimating these birds: seventy-nine kills were documented. Fortunately, the surviving cranes shifted away from brushy bobcat habitat to grazed pastures where cover was insufficient for bobcats. Crane mortality accordingly fell. In 1992 the first eggs were produced. The forecast is for annual releases of 25 to 30 cranes until the population exceeds 100 adults and subadults.

Reintroduction techniques for fledged cranes were recently summarized by Mini Nagendran and her coauthors. They are as follows.

Abrupt releases — Release of captive-reared cranes without acclimation to the release site (herein termed abrupt releases) has consistently resulted in high mortality. The first sizable release of captive-reared cranes occurred in 1971, when fourteen hand-reared Florida sandhill cranes were released by Nesbitt in south-central Florida without acclimation. None of the fourteen integrated into the wild flock, and within a few months all had died of exposure, starvation, or accident.

Following the Florida experiment, abrupt releases of parent-reared greater sandhill cranes were attempted at Grays Lake National Wildlife Refuge in 1976 (*n* = 1) and 1980 (*n* = 11). Of seven that survived to migrate south in 1980, none reappeared at Grays Lake the following spring. In 1984, Drewien released another twenty-one greater sandhill cranes at Grays Lake after they had been held in a small pen on site for four to six days; only nine (43%) survived to migrate.

Acclimated releases — For acclimated releases, the cranes are held at the release site two or more weeks, fed at the release site following release, and allowed to slowly acclimate to the release environment. Since 1981, more than a dozen acclimated releases have been made using parent-reared cranes from Patuxent. In nonmigratory situations, fifteen of twenty-seven (56%) Florida sandhill cranes survived their first winter and first year survival rates of 62% were achieved in Patuxent's early release program with Mississippi sandhill cranes.

A major improvement in the acclimated release process has been the rearing or training of chicks in the release area, allowing them opportunity to forage, encounter predators, and sometimes even interact with wild cranes. This type of rearing has been developed by Richard Urbanek with the human caretakers in costume and by Kent Clegg without costumes.

Miscellaneous methods — A variety of other reintroduction methods have been attempted with cranes. In Hokkaido, Japan, flightless male red-crowned cranes have lured wild females into their enclosures. The resulting pairs produced chicks that fledged into the wild flock. Occasionally, captive sandhill cranes have also attracted wild mates. A variation of this technique was tried twice with whooping cranes at Grays Lake. Because adult male whooping cranes in this experimental flock failed to obtain mates, two hand-reared females (one each in 1981 and 1989) were sent from Patuxent and introduced to the adult males. Both females were courted and while it appeared that bonds were forming, neither attempt resulted in eggs or in pairs that migrated together.

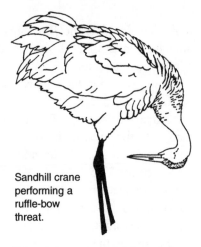

Sandhill crane performing a ruffle-bow threat.

Another variation of captive x wild pairing occurred in northern China: white-naped and red-crowned crane chicks were hand-reared and gradually released in the marshes at Zhalong. The birds were then returned to captivity to prevent their loss in the coming winter. In subsequent years, these semi-domestic birds paired with each other or with wild mates and nested in the marshes near their natal area. Young were generally kept in captivity with their parents the first winter. These birds joined the wild birds during the following year. Offspring resulting from these tame-wild matings were reportedly much more tolerant of human approach and consequently better able to live in a human-dominated environment.

An Overview of Hand-rearing verses Parent-rearing — During the past two decades, many attempts have been made to release small numbers of captive-reared cranes of several species around the world. Hand-reared birds at first proved unsuitable for reintroduction due to their reluctance to associate with wild conspecifics. As a result, most recent releases have involved rearing birds in pens with their natural or surrogate parents. These parent-reared birds proved to be much wilder than hand-reared birds and consequently were better able to adapt to the wild. Parent-reared cranes learn some foraging skills from their parents. Unfortunately, parent-rearing requires maintaining a captive flock of foster parents. Care of crane chicks is also much more difficult in field pens, and parent-rearing increases the risk of disease, parasite infestation, exposure to weather extremes, predation, and accidents.

It is important that release chicks be reared by conspecifics (i.e., parents or foster parents of their same species). Chicks reared by paired adults of their same species, showed proper sexual imprinting. However, four sandhill crane chicks reared at the International Crane Foundation by other species preferred the foster species when yearlings.

The hand-rearing technique used for this study is based on costume-rearing first begun in the 1960s at Patuxent, developed for release birds by Rob Horwich in the mid 1980s, modified for use with larger numbers of cranes by Richard Urbanek, and later adapted specifically for our trucking experiments.

With all of the recent developments in crane conservation, we expect that by the year 2000 all of the necessary arrangements will be complete to begin migratory flocks. Releases are expected to be somewhere near the Great Lakes (Wisconsin or Manitoba seems the most likely breeding site) with the birds wintering in Florida.

If future releases are at latitudes where no wild whooping cranes now live, the release birds must somehow be led south to preferred wintering sites. Obviously the techniques required to lead the birds south are critically important. Several experiments have begun with nonendangered sandhill cranes to serve this need. The first was our 1995 trucking experiment described in this volume (with some anecdotes also included from later experiments). Other experiments include 1995, 1996, and 1997 ultralight experiments led by Kent Clegg, an Idaho farmer and crane aficionado with nearly two decades of experience handling cranes. Kent's 1997 experiment was the first to involve whooping cranes (four birds) and would in itself, if allowed to continue, result in the establishment of a small number of whooping crane pairs breeding in the Rocky Mountains. In 1997, Bill Lishman and Joe Duff, founders of Operation Migration, switched from geese to cranes and led a small flock from central Ontario to eastern Virginia. All teams are poised to continue experiments and participate in actual whooping crane reintroduction attempts.

With this lengthy introduction, we are now ready to begin the adventure.

Chapter 6

The Migration

It is so easy, so free of emotion, to simply state that our migration began on October 2nd. This statement belies the agony we went through trying to decide when to go. How I envied the parent crane! It doesn't wonder, it just heads south when it feels right. We felt that it would feel right to a parent crane to head south when the first hard frost killed the grasshoppers. But, when would that happen? Not knowing, we planned for 2 October: as it turned out, a heavy frost made our choice a good one. As the odyssey unfolds in the following pages, you may wonder if our choice of a departure date was our only good decision.

For the last two weeks of September, I had been borrowing a craniac or two at a time to traverse the route with me so that all would be somewhat familiar with the hazards when we headed south with the cranes pressing at our heels. I also made up "trip-tiks," photocopied map strips with 20% overlap on which I had marked all stop signs, traffic signals, the worst mudholes, and powerlines. On our training trips, the crew members would compare the landscape with their maps and make personal notes indicating maximum speeds for certain hazards, rough spots, and corners. By the time we headed south with the cranes, all six participating personnel had traversed all or nearly all of the route once, and the three primary drivers had covered the route two or more times.

On one of these familiarization trips, some of the guys left the route and spent the evening at my home in the Santa Catalina Mountains, then worked on the radio bands the next day before returning to Camp Navajo. That evening they all enjoyed meeting Lothvar, my then 35-year-old golden eagle. After dinner, they discovered a jar we have had around the house many years: it contains perhaps 300 scorpions and a score of black widow spiders. Some of the guys seemed a little alarmed when they learned that many of these were collected inside the house. I also showed them a smaller bottle containing forty-nine scorpions collected during a single year, all from inside the house. They also learned that Cathy and I have been stung twice each while asleep in bed. With that information stored in their long-term memory banks, I suppose all of them had a little trouble bedding down on the floor that night. However, only one, Matt Shawkey, opted for sleeping in the bed of the pickup truck.

The sixth person on our migration crew was my friend of twenty-five years, Floyd Benjamin Potter Trahan, Jr., my same age, and more boisterous and talkative than any of the much younger crew. Ben had driven a lot of roads requiring four-wheel drive, most of it in two-wheel-drive vehicles. Although by October 1995, he claimed to be reformed, he still had no aversion to doing two-wheel-drifts around corners, and four-wheel-drifts could be expected if even the slightest emergency suggested the need. Although he claims that the opposite is true, my recollections from the 1970s are that it was me who was white-knuckled to the dash when he drove. Ben occupies a position as a computer programmer, where I am sure he does a fine job, but my belief is that he really belongs at a university, teaching philosophy, exposing the fallacies of our time. Because he is now deeply into psychological self evaluation, and does not fear peer pressure, he brought his "never-had-one-as-a-kid" teddy bear along for the migration. As a child, I had a teddy bear so I found his bear (or rather its presence on this expedition) rather odd.

On 2 October, all was ready. Ben and I joined the group at camp an hour later than expected because we had to find an unsqueamish person with a large freezer. On our journey north to Flagstaff, we had the good fortune to happen upon a road-killed raccoon with its eyes still firm (the criterion that must be met before I will stoop to salvaging carcasses . . . unless my eagle is very hungry). Further, we were able to add to our roof rack cache a cottontail and a coyote, both of which had died suddenly of lead poisoning.

Our trek south had been planned in detail. Three vehicles were involved. The cranemobile would normally be in the middle. The lead-car would be either my vintage '76 Scout or the U.S. Air Force pickup of unknown vintage obtained as surplus by the Fish and Wildlife Service and loaned to the project by the Buenos Aires National Wildlife Refuge. The lead-vehicle would carry two stop signs on poles, two orange vests, and two road crew type helmets. Each crane received a leg-band transmitter some days earlier, so the following-car and lead-car would have radio receivers to listen for errant cranes. All three vehicles would have a two-way radio, a set of maps, and, in case they really got lost, my wife's phone number.

The role of the lead-vehicle was to advise of traffic conditions, announce hazards, and most importantly, clear intersections so the cranemobile could rush through with unabated speed. This required that the lead-driver and navigator don vests and helmets as they approached an intersection, spring out of their truck, and take command of the intersection before the cranemobile shot past or the motorists realized that we were neither construction workers nor state-appointed officials.

The following-vehicle trailed the cranemobile by about 200 yards with the navigator in this third car either recording data or announcing, into his two-way radio, data concerning ground speed, altitude of cranes, etc., for the recorder who could be in any car. The best crane watching was from the following-car. The following-car also kept the driver of the cranemobile (whose vision of the birds was blocked by the 30 cubic yard box immediately behind his head) informed of the cranes' whereabouts. Finally, the following-car sometimes had to drop back to search for delinquent cranes.

At 2:30 p.m. the migration began. Because no road connected the trails on Camp Navajo to the Forest Service road heading south, we set out to walk the flock through two and a half miles of forest before beginning the first flight. Five of the cranes, familiar with the area, grew weary of hiking and flew back to camp. Part of the crew hiked back, loaded the five into the cranemobile, and brought them to us on the bumpy trail. When they arrived, they learned that four of the remaining five had also flown back to camp, so we chose to regather the birds at camp and truck them the long circuitous route to the Forest Service road. It was very frustrating for me to learn that our cranes were so independent. The only bird that was still with us when we arrived at the Forest Service fence was Z-Z. This crane had, until a few days previous, been our most adventurous, least attentive (to us) crane. Then she got lost on a training flight. When she was found, she had no desire to lose her foster parents again.

Two hours later, we unloaded the cranes on Garland Prairie. After a short rest at a pond, we gathered the cranes at the road edge, began waving and shouting, and drove away. All birds launched and followed the cranemobile, but by then the sun had already set, so after only two miles, we stopped on the open prairie, reluctant to lead the cranes into the forest in the approaching darkness. As we began to set up camp in the fading light, we inadvertently flushed the birds before they were penned, and as they circled in the fading light, we were unable to call four of them back to camp. What to do? Ben and I jumped in the Scout and rushed back two miles to the pond where we started flying. No cranes to be seen. Brian and Yoshi loaded their sleeping gear into the Air Force pickup and returned to Camp Navajo with the radio telemetry equipment. That night we stewed, bemoaning my decision to accept the free solar transmitters which were of no use after sunset.

On Garland Prairie, we penned five of the six remaining cranes. Schizoid, ultra-subordinate, paranoid Dennis we left out of the pen, not so much hoping she would fly away, but rather for her own sanity. With darkness, chilly air settled over the prairie: four of us huddled close to the crackling fire with five cranes in the pen and Dennis lurking in the shadows. What would tomorrow bring?

At 5 a.m. it was just getting light as I started to scan for our lost cranes. A thick crust of frost on my sleeping bag helped me decide to conduct my vigil from within. At 6:02 a.m., one lost crane walked into camp, and two more were spotted walking on the prairie 100 yards south. At 6:16 a.m., I saw a fourth crane flying about a half mile to the southeast. We jumped up, shouted, and called, and the tenth crane flew into camp. Ben and I sped back to Camp Navajo to alert Brian and Yoshi that we were calling off the search. We all zoomed to Garland Prairie, broke camp, lured the birds to the road, and then all three vehicles drove away with the cranes standing stupidly at the road edge.

We were a quarter mile west before they lifted off. They quickly caught up, and within two miles, we left the prairie and plunged into the forest. The birds were doing great: 200 feet up and matching our turns in the road perfectly. Only three miles into the forest, we arrived at the first stop sign of the trip. Curt and Ben in the lead-car stood in the intersection in orange vests and helmets, with stop signs at the ready. I blasted through in the cranemobile. Things couldn't be better, but a half mile later, we had no idea where the flock went. I called for a halt: we all jumped out calling and waving. All ten cranes circled over the forest canopy, dropped down through the trees, and alighted, ready for a drink and a bite of food.

After a half hour rest, we climb back into the trucks, and flapping and squawking, drive off. This time the cranes are eager to follow, and soon we are lumbering along with the cranes just above the forest canopy.

After only two miles, all ten veer sharply south and just disappear. It is our turn to stand in the road looking stupid. What to do? We assemble our radio telemetry equipment and begin the search. Within the hour, we find Miles, the leg dangler, at the road edge, alone and peeping for his human mama. I congratulate myself for not allowing CNN to film our expedition. Imagine how it would sound on the news. "The craniacs are now a full day into the migration, the cranes have flown an amazing ten miles, have gotten lost three times, and this team of extraordinary scientists still retain 10% of their flock."

The leg-band radios send back a "beep, beep, beep" from somewhere through the forest to the south. We split into three teams and search. One team hikes two miles to the head of Sycamore Canyon, one of God's most beautiful creations. When we are on the north side of the canyon, the signal says the cranes are south, but when we cross to the south side, the signal says the cranes are north. Anybody who has done fieldwork with radio telemetry knows this trick. What we have been following for two hours is the radio signal reflected off the canyon walls. But which wall and which way? We choose north, and hike until near sunset. Finally we realize the signal is coming from (probably reflected from) a tall hill. Three of us climb the hill, see Garland Prairie two miles east, and check our receiver. Yes, the signal is very strong from Garland Prairie. We gather the scattered troops, and streak back to the Prairie.

As it is too dark for solar leg bands to transmit, we all return to the previous night's campsite, turn our attention to our second most schizo bird, leg-dangler Miles, and act cheerful, each of us trying to avoid thinking that this project which has consumed much of our summer, is shaping up to be a ridiculous failure. Well, we have got one bird, a nice campfire, a warm sleeping bag, and elk are bugling in the forest to the southeast. Things could be a lot worse. Tomorrow we will find our birds and try again.

Day 3: 4 October. Sunrise at 6:30 a.m., 30°F, an eighth of an inch of ice in the soup pot, and one crane in camp. At least we still have six guys and all three trucks are working. We break into teams, begin scouting, and at 8:56 five cranes circle down and land near Curt and Yoshi at the west end of Garland Prairie. At 9:45, one more crane drops in. Now we have seven and among these are all three males. What to do? I decide that we will not give up, but will spend the rest of the day searching. Earlier, as we were zooming around coordinating teams, a front tire on the cranemobile had gone flat. Steel wires were exposed for half of the circumference . . . cursed, under-funded, government project. Nothing to do but for Ben and I to excuse ourselves, take a run to Williams, discover that prices are indeed higher in small towns, drive the thirty miles to Flagstaff, and get a proper tire.

While we were gone, two more cranes dropped in, the much maligned Dennis and Meerta, Matt's favorite. Only 116 is missing. This gentle, sleek, silver-gray, gorgeous bird is a favorite with every-one. At 5:45 that evening, I decide we have waited long enough. We load the cranes and drive along yesterday's flown route and cut south another eleven miles until we are out of the tall forest and into the piñon-juniper woodlands. We calculate that we should be able to keep the birds in sight over this shorter forest, so we pull fifty feet off the road and camp. Very quickly we wrap a net around a small clump of piñon and juniper trees, herd the cranes inside, provide them with food and water, then tend to our own needs.

One odd thing about our crew is that they all (except Ben and me) cook separately. Yoshi cooks kinda Japanese, Curt is a vegetarian, Brian likes Top Ramen (if you watch sales you can buy these for only 10 cents a packet). While Ben and I were getting the new tire earlier in the day, we loaded up on MEGA cans at a bargain food store so most

43

days from now on we would open a mega-pear, mega-peaches, or mega-pudding can.

As the evening wears on, my thoughts focus on our troubles. Why did the cranes twice break away when all was progressing well? I remember the eagles we had seen at three locations as we gathered our cranes. The golden eagle is, of the 9,000 species of birds that grace our world, by far my favorite. Little did I know what important role this special bird was to play in the days ahead.

Day 4: 5 October. Awake at dawn. We are now well below the frosty pine forests so it is much easier to get going. By 7:36 a.m., we pull onto the road to begin the best day of the trip.

We glide along paved roads with well-rounded curves, all downhill. The cranes slip easily through the air: we must travel 45-50 mph to stay ahead of them. Halfway down the hill, a canyon opens on the left, and Brian spots a golden eagle circling in toward the cranes. Our little flock veers abruptly to the right, but stays close to the cranemobile. Ahead, the pavement ends and we must wind on very rough roads across a narrow canyon. Ben and I speed ahead and prepare to call down the cranes. As the cranemobile and the other car approaches, we see our birds are looking trim and fit, so I make a quick decision. I call for everybody to stay in their cars and go for it. As the cranes circle overhead, our little convoy enters the canyon, bounces across the wash bed, then up onto the far rim. We all bolt from our cars and run squawking and flapping into the open. The birds circle again and again. We expect them to be tired, but they are ready for more. After five more minutes, they circle down and land all about us. We rest and water them for a half hour, then start up our engines. The birds come to attention. We're off, flapping and squawking our way west to Hell Canyon.

On the way, the road crosses two powerline corridors just as the lines cross each other. The result is something of a hazard, so Ben and I, in the lead-car, pull ahead to watch the passage. The cranemobile is approaching with a cloud of dust at its heels. The cranes form an undulating line 150 feet above and a little behind the cranemobile as it passes under the wires. The cranes pass above the two-phase 230 KV line, but are at the same height as the conductors on the 500 KV line. The tension rises. The lead bird passes over the wires, the trailing birds are lower and will pass under, but the intervening birds flip sideways as

44

they pass between the wires. Our 40, a beautiful, gray female, flares to miss the line. As she does so, both legs slap against the conductor. She tumbles, then plummets downward. We look back and sicken at the sight. Then she regains control, levels out, and pumps frantically trying to catch up with her flock mates. It appears she is gaining on the flock, but then we notice that both legs are dangling and blood seems to be dripping from her legs. For three long miles, she valiantly pumps along, then begins to lose her battle to join the flock. Slowly she drops back, then sets her wings and glides down into the juniper forest. The flock, in seeming sympathy, circles back, divides into two groups, and drops slowly into the junipers. We in the vehicles circle back, dig out the radio telemetry equipment and spend the next half hour triangulating on cranes scattered through the woods. Yoshi follows one signal back into the junipers and finds 40 lying on the ground in the shade of a small juniper.

At first he radios us that she is okay, but as he lifts her, he feels the blood running from her legs. Yoshi quietly announces, "Looks like leg broken." I leave Brian and his team with three cranes and rush through the forest to join Yoshi. Yes, not only one, but both legs are broken. Over the two-way radio, Brian and I discuss our options. Cranes with even one broken leg seldom survive even with the best veterinary care. I agree with Brian's assessment . . . we should end her suffering. At both ends of the radio link, all converse and concur. I ask Yoshi to carry 40 to a juniper stump. With heavy heart he does so as I walk with dread to my four-wheel-drive and draw my machete from under the carpet. Yoshi cradles the crane. Robert Doyle extends the crane's neck over the stump, and the blade flashes down. Death is instantaneous.

We reassemble our flock. The cloud of mourning dispels somewhat. We rise and prepare to cross Hell Canyon. Although the canyon is about 800 feet deep, it is a lot less like hell than many canyons in Arizona. To approach the rim of the canyon, we must first maneuver about 500 yards of a cactus-riddled, juniper woodland. The craniacs all walk very carefully to avoid prickly pear cactus spines, but the cranes seem to naturally avoid these hazards without concern.

My plan at Hell Canyon is for Brian and me to wait on the canyon rim with the cranes while the rest of the guys drive two vehicles on a four and a half mile loop to the north and back to the west side of the canyon where they will lure the birds across once Brian and I get them airborne. In about thirty minutes, the four craniacs are in position to the west with two vehicles. Brian and I call a loud gargling whoop, the sandhill crane ready-to-go-squawk. The cranes are immediately heads-up, then as Brian and I run and flap toward the canyon, the cranes fall in behind us. Brian and I jump just over the upper rim of the canyon and slide deftly out of sight behind great basalt boulders so that the cranes will focus on our compatriots across the canyon. The plan works. The cranes pass over our heads, circle over the canyon, then soar for five to ten minutes until one by one they float down to join the craniacs a quarter of a mile away and 200 feet below.

With the cranes safely across, Brian and I race to the Scout and speed to the far side of the canyon. After an hour resting the cranes and walking them to Highway 89, we all sit in the shade of a juniper, as trucks roar past at speeds well over the legal limit. How were we going to get the birds going without endangering them, us, and the locals? Having already lost one lovely crane: how can we avoid losing another? We move all three cars down onto the edge of the road. Ben and I walk onto the rim of the road cut looking down twenty feet at the highway. The cranes follow and with a little coaxing, we get them through the barbed wire fence. We wait until we have an opening in the traffic, then two of our trucks start moving and pull ahead of us. Brian toots his whistle and waves frantically from the rear of the cranemobile. Ben and I begin running and flapping and squawking in Brian's direction: the cranes sprint along behind. Ben and I jump over the rim of the road cut and slide down to the highway. The cranes take their cue and fall in behind the cranemobile. Ben and I scramble into my Scout and we are soon catching up to our troops.

The birds climb to 200 feet and although cars zoom past us coming and going, we are making good progress. Our excitement rises despite the lingering shadow of our recent loss. Three miles pass, then five. As we begin the slow climb over a long juniper-covered ridge, the crane's trajectory converges with the slope of the hill. In horror, I watch as a pickup truck speeds over the hill toward us just as the birds veer onto the roadway. Over my shoulder and in a split second, I calculate the height of the birds, assess the potential for impact. My brain forecasts a collision. Ben grabs the wheel as I turn to watch the outcome. The leading cranes see disaster coming and veer away, but the last bird flares barely ahead of the oncoming truck. Its legs pendulate downward within two feet of the truck's windshield. I squawk on the radio, "Let's pull over and regroup." Our little convoy veers to the right and we all rush about assembling our migrants. I call for a conference, then vent my fears. I am at an emotional nadir. The craniacs form a circle, and, as if also wishing to participate in the discussions, the cranes form a ring around us. I ask for opinions. An hour ago we lost a bird, and now we have nearly arranged for a windshield collision. The crane almost surely would have died, and we are loath to think what could have happened to the driver. What right have we, have I, to jeopardize life and limb? I recommend we "throw in the towel: why continue to execute what was from the beginning a bad idea." The guys, each in turn, express themselves. My friends feel it is worth the try. We can be more careful. We are almost to the rim of the plateau. We should continue on. The cloud dispels somewhat, optimism returns. We rise, position our flock, and start off. From the plateau top it is a long slow glide down into Chino Valley. The cranes rest on the wing as they make their descent.

As we approach the valley floor, the cranes climb to about 700 feet which confuses the cranemobile driver (who will remain un-named) and causes him to slow down, causing one crane to drop down to join the truck. Simultaneously, Brian's police whistle (which had long ago replaced his overtaxed vocal cords as the instrument of choice when conversing with the flying cranes) stimulates a boxer dog to rush from its residence 100 yards from the road. So . . . the cranemobile driver stops because it looks like the crane is going to land: the crane lands on the pavement because the cranemobile stops: the dog rushes to the whistle because that's what he was trained to do: Brian jumps out of the cranemobile to attack the dog because he can't help himself, and the traffic stops because they don't know what else to do. Then two craniacs (who will not be named) throw rocks at the dog, pounce on a very puzzled 109, load it into the cranemobile, and speed away while eight other cranes soar overhead. The uninvolved motorists gawk and think . . . "Can't say I've seen that happen around here before." Once this flight is over, it will be my job to disentangle the causes of the event and prevent similar occurrences.

I have often marveled how an unanticipated and fleeting event can change our lives forever: produce an incident which will never be understood, create a memory which will never be forgotten.

Fortunately, this ten-second anomaly in world history resulted in no crushed bodies (canine, gruine, or hominid), no twisted metal, and neither shattered glass nor shattered lives.

Just a few miles ahead, there is a lot of shattered glass on the highway, two crumpled cars, and a dozen or so undamaged cars are stopped on the road while their occupants rubberneck the scene. The only thing that draws human attention more efficiently than a swapmeet is a traffic accident. We have a flock of cranes overhead and we do not want them to land in the midst of a traffic spectacle so our convoy veers right, off the road, and bounces its way past the lookers-on. For a few seconds, the focus of the whole crowd, even the victims, shifts from the twisted metal to the flag-flying ambulance and the big birds attending it from on high. For a fleeting moment, a motorized migration replaces traffic accidents as "numero uno" on the list of human fascinations.

Safely around the traffic accident, we speed on for another four miles and land our cranes at the north end of Sullivan Buttes, fifty feet from the locked gate marking the perimeter of the John Punchcow ranch.

It's noon. As we wait, watering our cranes and wishing for more shade than the cranemobile can provide, a cowboy rides up in a pickup and opens the Punchcow gate. I stride quickly to his side, hoping my unwashed body and weird costume will not offend. He very attentively listens to my desires to continue west, laments Mr. Punchcow's uncooperative stance, locks the gate, and then drives away. Okay guys, let's load 'em up.

With all cranes safely aboard, we drive back east to begin the 40-mile circuit to the other side of the Punchcow ranch. In Paulden, we stopped for fuel and a cool treat. Almost without exception, everyone we meet at roadside stops wants to know why we are driving a MASH wagon and why the strange attire. Few believe, without a peek in the big box, that the real reason for our strange clothing, vehicles, and behavior is that our truck harbors a flock of cranes.

At the start of the next leg, we are now far enough west of the Bradshaw Mountains to finally start directly south. It is 2:20 p.m.: we are on the open prairie at the west edge of the Punchcow ranch. The birds are rested, watered, fed, and ready to fly south into Skull Valley. At 2:23 p.m., they lift off. The birds have flown thirty miles today and are really behaving like a team. They flap along at about 200 feet forming a long undulating line. Unbeknownst to the cranes, a prairie falcon is resting on a powerline tower directly ahead. Like a football team closing in to prevent the punt return, the cranes converge on the metal tower. The falcon gets very sleek and calls for a fair catch, but the ten cranes inexorably, unflaggingly close in. The falcon panics, forgets that it is all a game, and flaps frantically to the side.

On the mid-afternoon thermals, the cranes climb to about 1,000 feet and glide south parallel to the cranemobile. After about three miles, a raven begins pursuing the flock: no problem. Eight miles go by and we turn southwest onto Fair Oaks Road. Dust and gravel spray as we skid around the first corner. The road has too many corners, the cranes drop down and match our turns. They are only forty feet above the ground, and we are really working to stay ahead of them on the windy road.

Ben and I, in the lead-car, notice that no one is behind us. We stop, wait five minutes. Nope, no one is coming. We retrace our route, and at mile 79 we see our troops (cranes and craniacs) gathered at the road side. The cranes are looking around unconcerned, one pecks at a grasshopper, two peck at nothing but the dirt. Our team members are huddled close together examining something on the ground. We walk closer: it is gray, smells of burnt feathers, and is very dead. Crane 89, one of our big males, lies there, just as beautiful as a few moments before. Brian and the four craniacs saw it happen. As the flock passed through the low voltage distribution line that joined us two miles earlier, 89, in the rear, veered too late, collided, and fell limp without a struggle. This "last bird is vulnerable" pattern is becoming quite clear.

Much of our flight training at Camp Navajo was designed to prevent this. What went wrong? Though we many times flew our birds through powerlines so they would learn to avoid collisions, we were never convinced that they were really educated. The lead birds always seemed to detect the lines and swerve away, but we always felt that the last birds were just following the earlier birds and not watching for hazards. We had often seen the last birds flare and nearly collide, much like the last car in a chain collision really has no time to react. This is our second powerline fatality.

There was nothing to do but stow 89 in a truck with 40 for a necropsy that night, and go on. The eight remaining birds fell quickly into formation. We were all shaking our heads, stunned at the loss of 89, a very valuable bird, a chick that the craniacs had reared and trained and watched develop since hatching. The beauty of the high rolling hills, the oak savanna, and the thin line of cranes following us 500 feet aloft lessened our distress.

We continue south, everything is apparently perfect, then Matt squawks on the radio, "There's a large black bird approaching the cranes." One glance over my left shoulder and I know in an instant what is happening. An adult, probably female, golden eagle folded like a fighter jet, is plunging earthward toward our tiny flock. In one movement, I hit the brakes, bark for my rifle, and hand the steering wheel to Ben. Before the car stops skidding, I am standing by the dirt road firing shot after shot toward my favorite species. The eagle, recovering from her stoop through the flock, shoots up, stalls, then begins circling back as if for another try at the now scattered cranes. She hears the quick barking of my rifle, listens as tiny lead projectiles whiz past, turns quickly away from the cranes, and makes for the eastern horizon, Granite Mountain. She was never really threatened by my shots. I have never killed an eagle and made sure my slugs were well wide of the mark.

Even before I finish shooting, the cranes begin raining around me into the scrubby vegetation at the road edge. This brushy hillside is anything but crane habitat, but once again, the cranes are glad to be near Mother. Matt walks up and thanks me for saving his cranes. I take no credit, and as we eventually learn, it is actually the speed and maneuverability of these cranes, even though they are juveniles, that makes them a good match for even an adult eagle.

Relieved to think we may actually have some effect during an eagle attack and pleased to see that our little charges are able to avoid the eagle's lethal talons, we water our flock and head south. The road twists and turns, climbs and plunges, but we are progressing well. We have the birds right on our tail when the cranemobile passes under a railroad trestle. No problem: car under, birds over.

Our last hurdle for the day is the climb up to the paved road heading south and downhill into the little hamlet of Skull Valley. Once the cranemobile is on the pavement, our cranes decide to show us what they can do. They catch rising air, spiral up to about 2,000 feet, then soar along behind us. Finally, about a half mile north of the village, our little flock begins drifting east with the wind. All three trucks pool up at the road edge. We stand there flapping and calling until the troop starts back in our direction.

Now the rush is on to get back on the road and give the cranes an object to follow before they think of something else to do. I am in the Scout behind the cranemobile: we rush ahead to show the other craniacs the side road to the Dave Jenner ranch. No time to waste as we blast into the one-gas-station, one-store town of Skull Valley. Unfortunately, we forgot to warn the populace that we were coming. Three teenage girls stand in the road exchanging pleasantries with a pickup load of boys. All are blocking our turn to the south. The horn on my Scout does not work, so only our movements will tell these girls what to do. As we plunge forward, I can read these girls like an optometrist's chart. The girl on the left is clearly going to jump left, the one on the right will snuggle right against the boy's truck, and the girl in the middle (who is directly in our path) is going to jump both ways. We in the lead-car detect only terror as we sweep by. The cranemobile, second around the corner, sees nervous tee-hee-hee's, and by the time the following-car slips around the corner, laughter has replaced thoughts of lawsuits.

Visions of near mayhem fading in our rear view mirror, we gun the Scout toward the Jenner boundary. There will be no time to saunter quietly down Mr. Jenner's cottonwood lined lane, no time to announce our arrival. The birds are too high and too loose for us to focus on anything but getting them down fast. My Scout skids to a dusty halt at the road edge. I spring over the fence with Ben plunging along at my rear. We race into the open meadow, screaming and waving to the flock 1,500 feet overhead. Soon the other cars arrive. One, two, then three other craniacs join us. We stand there, each of us in our own little whirlwind of thoughts. They thinking how stupid we will look if the cranes do not come down, how stupid we already look flapping and squawking, and me thinking how glad I am that I told CNN to get lost. The cranes carve circle after lazy circle in the warm afternoon sky. Why go down to the overheated surface? What earthly reward could compensate for this celestial view? Why land in a dusty, cowpie-dotted field? Then, the answer came to them. Mama. Crane baby wants mama.

51

One crane starts down, plunging through the intervening space. Another takes its lead. Then I notice: Hell! We are in the wrong field. Like a prison escapee, I sprint for the fence, put two hands on the top wire, and sail over, barking my invitation for my fellow craniacs to join me, pronto.

Swoop, flail, plop: swoop, flail, flop. The cranes one by one drop at our feet. All of them. Soon we are all grinning and congratulating ourselves and the birds. Brian Clauss slowly, deliberately, walks over to me, holds out his hand. I look into his dusty face, look at his dusty legs, dusty arms, and focus my thoughts. I think how much I appreciate his volunteering to ride the whole route, especially the dirt-covered back roads in the back of the open cranemobile with the dust billowing all about. Brian shakes my hand, "Congratulations. I now think it is possible." I shake back, but I am thinking, "Of course it's possible. All you have to do is wave your arms, squawk in the right language, and most importantly, you had to be there when the little guys were learning what their mama looks like."

Even with the loss of 89 and 40, it is a joyous evening as we prepare to camp with our eagle-eluding aerial athletes. Today we covered seventy-two miles, and the cranes flew nearly all of that. It is a time for congratulations and yes, we all now believe, even know, it is possible.

It was only 4:25 p.m. when our birds lit, so I hopped into the Scout and rushed to announce our arrival to our host. Mr. Jenner turned out to be a silver-haired, slim but healthy, slightly bent, octogenarian. He seems alert and eagerly accepts my invitation to become a short-term craniac. Donning the red cap and an anorak, he walks with me into the field to greet the cranes and my team.

Whooping crane performing a butterfly threat.

Fortunately, courtesy in America does not require us to join him at tea or him to stay for cocoa. Instead, we share a happy, cordial half hour with all parties gratified and no one bored. My memories turn to a time and a land far away when I was the only American and the only nondrinker sitting for hours as my Russian hosts drank themselves silly. The words of my acquaintance Professor Vladimir Flint, in some circles considered the dean of Russian ornithology, come to mind. As he raised yet another toast, he turned aside and whispered to me, "Ridiculous Russian custom." Thank heaven for the simple, friendly, courtesy we, as Americans, exchange, then part to our several separate interests: Dave Jenner to counting cattle expenditures, me to a necropsy on 89.

We choose our campsite well. Aged cottonwoods dangle weathered limbs over us, blotting out the hot afternoon sun as we prepare for the evening. The cranes are, of course, interested in the bugs attending each cowpie. Unfortunately, they are even more interested in us. As they poke about camp, nothing is safe from their bill jabs or deposits from the other extremity. Our solution? We erect the net that last night encircled the cranes and use it to close the gaps between our circled cars: people in, cranes out. Tonight, we sleep in the pen. Brian and Curt take it a step further, and arrange their gear on the roof of the cranemobile.

What's for dinner? We need something to celebrate our first day of real progress down the road. First, we have to do the necropsy before it gets dark. With most hominoid eyeballs focused on the hood of the Air Force truck, I make a long incision to see why 89 died so quickly. No broken neck, some bleeding by one ear, looks like the major injury is a broken thigh. I am no vet, but my guess is that sudden death resulted from electrocution when the crane bridged the gap between two conductors. The job complete, I wonder what to do with a dead crane. Matt thinks the feathers are beautiful and wants to save some. Brian comments, "On the farm we ate stuff when it died." My mind slips back almost forty years to a night-time electrical storm at my folks' farm near Steamboat Springs, Colorado. Morning revealed a heap of fifty fryers suffocated in one corner of the chicken house. It wasn't difficult to decide what to do that morning, and it wasn't difficult to decide what to do this evening either. Someone found a can of stewed tomatoes: someone else carved the meat that would stew with it. Later that night, Matt and Curt buried the remains deep in the sandy wash bed fifty yards from camp.

With darkness came the discovery that there really is a good reason why normal people put the sheep in the pen while the shepherd sleeps nearby. Two very hungry great horned owls showed up at dusk and their preference for sitting on poles within fifty yards of camp prompted us to dig out another net and encircle the cranes also.

Perhaps emboldened by the events of the day, perhaps exhilarated by the tasty dinner, or perhaps just lonesome, Ben broke out his teddy bear. Whereas we had previously caught only fleeting glimpses of this cuddly prize, tonight was Ben's "coming out" party. Tonight Bear was sleeping in plain view right next to Ben. Hey! What's the purpose of a teddy bear if not to brighten one's life? And Ben's courage in not concealing "Bear" brightened our faces as well. Yoshi, head steeped in oriental reserve, was hard to read under these circumstances.

Maybe it was Ben's bear, but that night the climate seemed right for some intimacy, so as we relaxed around the campfire, I suggested we swap stories about our most embarrassing moments. Yoshi, who is really very good in English, told us about a disastrous exchange he had years ago with the intercom at a drive-in, fast food joint. Though he tried again and again, pronouncing "l's" was beyond the capabilities of his Japanese tongue. He simply could not convince the machine that he wanted a vanilla shake. Everyone laughed heartily at Yoshi's predicament, but I secretly believed that either life has treated Yoshi very kindly or he had a few other more embarrassing moments that he wasn't sharing with us.

On the other hand, Brian's story was about as bad as it can get. Seems he was one evening at a munchies and beer party at a private home when to his surprise an absolutely gorgeous girl fell into conversation with him. He stood there, chatting away, amazed that he, generally abashed around good-looking women who normally avoid him anyhow, was able to do so well swapping pleasantries with this beauty. Between turns talking, he happened to set his beer mug on the table next to that of another. When he took it up again, he had a heavy waft half way down his throat before he noticed that he was swallowing not only the dregs of someone else's beer, but also a small number of matches and other ejecta that might be expected to take up residence in a castoff mug. Not wanting to destroy a beautiful moment, he, in an instant, decided not to gag and spit as any normal person would have done under similar circumstances. Rather, without showing a sign of the turmoil within, he maintained eye contact with his newfound friend and swallowed the mug's disgusting contents. The girl, a better observer than Brian, shrieked in disgust and departed posthaste. I guess the moral of the story is that under certain circumstances, it is advisable to gag, even if it may mess up the opportunity of a lifetime.

Not to be outdone by Brian, Matt Shawkey told us of a grade school disaster that nearly robbed him of his last vestige of self esteem. One wintery day, Matt, who had already endured years of abuse by larger, meaner classmates, was late arriving at the bus stop. When he rushed up, the bus was already pulling away, so he charged into the icy street and ran yelling after it. As Matt revealed his painful tale, I could see his classmates grinning from the bus, noses pressed to the glass, pointing and laughing. At length the bus driver got the word that the pencil-necked dweeb wanted to get on the bus, so she slid to a controlled stop. Matt, already running at full speed, had little time to react. He just plopped forward on his face and slid under the bus. My childhood was not so painless that I could not imagine his anguish as he extricated himself from beneath the yellow behemoth, climbed the stairs, then walked the gauntlet, past row after row of mocking, derisive peers. Glad I missed that one.

Now it was Ben's turn. He didn't want anyone to know his story, but he couldn't let Matt outdo him either. Ben is normally rather loquacious, so I was taken back a bit when with very little introduction he just blurted out that one day at a family gathering . . . well, you know how in the 60s boys used to wear their pants way low, about to fall off, almost like city kids today. Well, his sister by stealth sidled up to him, grabbed at mid-thigh and jerked his breeches down to his knees. We all howled knowing what a shock he must have felt. Then one in the fire-illuminated circle asked the obvious question. And yes, his undies thankfully stayed up.

Others around the campfire took their turn: Each one reliving their shame and the resulting derision. At last it was up to me to see if I could top them all. I should have just let Ben win, or maybe Matt's story was the best/ worst. Ah, who cares, I decided. I'll just blurt it out, then see if they all turn away in disgust.

I began, "Well, some of you know that at age sixteen I broke my back. So I was in the hospital for a couple of weeks before they put me in a cast and during the whole time I never once defecated. Spinal cord damage can change things, you understand. Don't be mistaken. They had fed me laxatives and tried enemas twice, but all to no avail. Well, uh, one day the very pretty girl came over to my bed. She was a candy striper. Do they still use that term? That's right, a nurse's helper. So this girl comes up to me very friendly-like and I could tell she wanted something and I could tell that I very much wanted to cooperate. By way of excusing myself, I should also say that I was also not so far from death, and if you die, presumably you don't have to be embarrassed anymore, so to get on with it, she asked me if I wouldn't mind if she gave me a 'grease enema.'" This whole incident is still so disgusting to me, I almost couldn't go on. "What she really wanted me to do was let her pass her test on enema giving by having her do it while three nurses watched to see if everything came out . . . er, uh, well, to see if she did okay." By now everyone in the circle could see where this tale of horror was leading, so I just blurted it out. "I said okay she could do it, and she came, and they came, and I rolled over, and she did it, and they watched, but even the grease didn't produce anything."

There, it's done. I look at the faces around the fire: I don't see the barely controlled mirth that came with everyone else's stories. All I see is blank horror, genuine disgust. I guess I won. I think.

Day 5: 6 October. Morning came a bit too early. As we rushed about disentangling our nets and stowing our gear, every so often someone would bark at a crane for stabbing a hole in his pillow or making a deposit on his sleeping tarp.

A slight problem began the day. We were camped in a field about 50 yards, three fences, a dirt road and a railroad track away from the paved road south. Life being too precious to spend on the mundane, I never even considered loading the cranes in the cranemobile and hauling them to the paved road. Rather, I decided on doing a crane "handoff." We proceeded as follows. As the rest of the team distracted the cranes, Matt and Brian moved the cranemobile into position on the paved road. Then we moved the other two vehicles into position in the cow pasture. Up went the flags, and off went Brian's whistle. The two trucks lumbered in a wide arc toward the cranemobile with four of us squawking and waving. The cranemobile, poised at the road edge, began to creep forward. The cranes, excited for another day, postured, then began running and flapping behind. Within five seconds, the two trucks would run out of space in the pasture, but by then the cranes were overhead, trying to catch up with the cranemobile. Spurred on by the flags and Brian's whistle, the cranes took their cue and dutifully followed the cranemobile down the paved road.

As soon as the cranes passed us, we in the other two trucks folded our "wings," stifled our squawks, and decelerated to a stop just before hitting the fence. When the cranes were out of sight down the road, we headed for the gate, lumbered down the shaded lane, crossed the dirt road, bounced up and over the railroad and onto the pavement. Once on the highway, we quickly caught up with our little migration, moved into our positions as lead and following-cars, contemplated inner peace, and settled into our routine. The radio squawked, "Cranes at 200 feet, speed 33 mph, time 8:37."

At the road edge, a shaggy-headed, wild-eyed, bicyclist pedals slowly up one of many hills. Like us, he must cross the Weaver Mountains and descend into the heat of the Sonoran Desert. I always wanted to interview one of these peregrinating pedalists: little did I know my wish was soon to be granted.

Our route south is mostly through scattered mesquites. We sweep past a cluster of white limestone spires and alcoves. The cranes are pumping along in "V" formation. Five miles go by quickly, and we find ourselves rushing through a tiny burg called Kirkland. There is a sharp left turn ahead, so Matt guns the cranemobile to sprint ahead so the cranes will not be confused as he slows for the turn. After two more tranquil miles (if you call it tranquil to spend your morning waving and squawking to birds overhead), it is "pay-back time." Ben and I spot a golden eagle on a powerline just at the edge of the road. I hand Ben the steering wheel, lean out the window, and focus on the impending encounter. The cranes are lined up in close-rank formation just above the powerlines and are pumping energetically toward the eagle. When the cranes are 100 yards away, the eagle sleeks, stares in disbelief at apparently being attacked by a flock of cranes, then bolts from his perch and flaps rapidly aside. I love to see raptors attack things, but am glad to forego that pleasure today. After the cranes pass, the eagle returns to his roadside perch.

A few more miles slide by and we start a 300-foot climb to the ridge top before descending into Peeples Valley. The cranes are pumping hard. They are not exhausted, just overheated. Bills agape, they come lower and lower as the landscape rises up to meet them. Not much oncoming traffic: that's good. All eyes strain to follow the cranes. A decision is needed: "Lead-car, pull out left and call them down." Before the plan can be fully executed, the birds begin plopping down immediately at the road edge next to the lead-car. We all walk quickly left calling the birds safely off the road. Yoshi grabs the bucket and jug. Glug, glug, glug . . . the bucket is two-thirds full and one by one, dominant before subordinate, the cranes dip and point upward, dip and point to refresh themselves. Among birds, only doves and sand grouse can drink without raising their bills. Too bad humans aren't like cranes . . . it would make for a lot more action at banquets and cocktail parties . . . dip and point.

A squirt bottle also comes out of my Scout. A lot of heat can be lost through a crane's long, bare legs so, starting with the crane that is panting the most, we spray each pair of legs until the cranes quit panting.

Seven miles behind us, the haggard cyclist wobbles up another nameless hill. None of the craniacs pay him any attention, or if they do, none of them imagine that they will ever, in this lifetime, see him again. Wrong.

The cranes recover quickly. None are fatigued, so we mentally ask them if they are ready to go on. They bustle about and tell us by their body language, "We're ready if you are." The Air Force pickup pulls to the crest of the hill and squawks, "Car coming." We wait. The car passes, the driver looks puzzled at our roadside assemblage, but continues north, cyclist bound. Air Force squawks, "Another car." We wait, the car passes, our short term memory banks erase the driver's wide-eyed visage as soon as he is out of sight down the hill. His long term memory bites deep into what he has just seen.

Air Force squawks, "All clear." Matt guns the cranemobile engine, Brian whistles, and the cranes are all heads up. Everyone slides quickly into his now-we-are-moving mode. It is 9:28 a.m., and we have an appointment with the hot winds rising from the Sonoran Desert.

Our little caravan moves forward. We have some excellent flights behind us, and hours of daylight ahead. It is easy to see the optimism in everyone's faces. We're doing it! I have often noticed that joviality can very quickly produce a superficial kind of friendship, a camaraderie that makes people meet often and do fun things together, while the basis for lasting, heart-melding friendship is true, faithful, and unbegrudging service during times of crisis. This migration would supply a plethora of opportunities for both types of social bonding.

Chapter 7

Gift of an Eagle

Traveling 35 mph with a flock of cranes in tow on a paved, two-way road while everyone else is going 60 mph is less hazardous than it sounds. If the motorists stay where they are supposed to and do not pool up behind the cranemobile enjoying the diversion from their otherwise craneless lives, everybody is going to survive. And the oncoming traffic actually benefits the migration by alarming the birds and making them fly higher. It is great fun watching not only the cranes, but also the faces of unsuspecting travelers. Vehicles approaching from behind have a good opportunity to see what is going on. Some actually scramble and dig for their video cameras. Oncoming traffic has less time to contemplate cranes and craniacs. They either just whiz past, dull-eyed and unnoticing, or bug-eyed and aching to know.

We top the ridge and glide briskly down into Peeples Valley, an attractive, well-watered, oak-surrounded diversion from the mesquite-covered hills at lower elevations. To the right we pass the Mountainaire Market. In my mind, I wave hello to an undesignated clerk, someone I have probably met on one of my many passages through this valley while scouting for the best migration route.

The road climbs again. Just another five miles and we will be over the Weaver Mountains. From there, we will drop down 3,000 feet into the Sonoran Desert. Just five more miles and the last serious climb of the expedition will be behind. The cranes are looking good. Miles is gaping as she flies, but Miles always gapes . . . the result of some child-hood disease.

We are climbing rapidly as we enter the outskirts of Yarnell, another one of Arizona 300-yard-long-business-strip villages, flanked left and right by dusty streets lined with modest homes and trailer houses. The cranes drop down to housetop level, but keep pumping along. We swiftly pass the rock shops, the motel, the eateries, and the antique (alias junk) shop. In the Scout, now in following-car position, I scan as best I can. A dozen cars mill about the streets, a dozen rustics trudge up or saunter down Main Street, not one eye lifts to behold the splendor of the world's first truck-led migration. Why are we doing this if people are not interested? Surely someone will turn to stare at the cranemobile, flags popping, as we pass. Surely Brian, bespectacled and strangely clad and even stranger behaved — looking skyward, tooting and waving his red cap in a monotonous cadence, will merit attention. But not one soul looks up. They had seen it all before, or more likely, they had long since given up on anything of Guinness Book genre ever passing through Yarnell, Arizona, population 250.

Almost at the very edge of Yarnell, our route plunges over the brink of the mountains. The hot breath of the Sonoran Desert assaults this escarpment, then deflects upward into the sky. Our cranes go with it. As soon as we top the ridge, all eight, almost without a flap, were raptured heavenward and soared in lazy circles, gawking at a handful of red-crowned craniacs staring skyward. Only the cranemobile, with its white crane silhouette painted on the roof and its two azure and black flags popping in the wind, holds any significance.

As per Plan A, we glide over the mountain crest and slide to a halt beside a trashed-out diner. Four of us sprint up a tiny hill and stand agape beside a small, white, rust-freckled, abandoned water tank. We call and wave, trying to lure the birds down. On the hot desert air, the cranes effortlessly and steadily climb into the sky. Plan A is not working. Three rather forlorn earthlings flap and squawk. A fourth earthling, Brian, flaps and blasts his whistle in our ears. Three of us call for acoustical relief. Brian moves 50 feet aside and blares on. Only Curt and Ben in the Air Force pickup are under the impression that we are still on Plan A. They are waiting for us a curve or two down the mountain.

The cranes circle. Parallax leaves us wondering if they were circling up or circling down. Two, five, ten more circles and we know.

Thankfully they are circling down. Our plan is to land the cranes at the white water tower, hold them there until the cranemobile can wind half way down the mountain, then release them to follow the cranemobile to the bottom where cranes and craniacs will reassemble for a post-descent celebration.

The celebration will have to wait. Ben squawks on his two-way radio, "There's an eagle down here." Without waiting for a reply, he pulls out the shotgun, loads it with a shell cracker, and launches the projectile eagle-ward. The projectile explodes just as planned near the eagle, and the eagle, just as would be expected, catches an updraft and climbs. As the eagle is going up, 86 begins plunging down from the flock. What to do? What to do?

Never having been a subscriber to the Eisenhower wait-and-see principle, I bark instructions, "To the vehicles. Let's go for it." So the eagle goes up, and the cranes come down. We rush down the mountain hoping the cranes will follow, Yoshi looks out the window of the Scout and sees a large dark object plummet from above and flash through the crane flock. That is all. The road is too windy. The birds are too far or quick or whatever. We just cannot see more. Even when we stop the Scout, climb out, and squint into the sun-dominated sky, we see no cranes and no eagle.

Curt radios, "We're down here at the pullout at the bottom of the mountain and we've got 86. Where are the other birds?" I answer, "Watch the skyline. We're coming down." Ten minutes later, we are all assembled at the Joshua tree at the base of the mountain. All the humanoids are assembled, that is. 86 is my favorite bird, and we are all glad to see him, but we are a little disappointed that he didn't bring his friends to the celebration.

It is 10 a.m., 80°F, and getting hotter by the minute. Time to doubt one's sanity. Time to keep one's thoughts hidden. Time for Ben to say, "Looks like it's time to leave the one and go after the ninety and nine." It is not time to tell Ben what I think of his humor.

Breaking out the radio telemetry equipment, we form teams. Curt and Yoshi take the Air Force truck on a radio telemetry trip around the base of the mountain. The remainder of us stand around watching ravens play along the ridge top 2,300 feet above. We're all wishing these ravens had long necks and long legs. A police car turns into the pullout. We are 100 feet away, but with the cranemobile, flags, and costumes, we look suspiciously like the most conspicuous drug runners he has ever seen. He approaches, I intercept, we talk. "Yeah, migrating cranes, yep that's one over there." 86 pecks at a broken beer bottle on the rocky hillside. "Might take awhile finding the others."

I did not actually describe the details of the process or how the cranes fly down the road behind us. The nice officer, hopes fading for an exciting day exchanging gun fire with a MASH wagon, never paid us enough mind to consider how it might blemish his reputation for a flock of cranes to follow a camouflaged ambulance across his territory.

Matt, Brian, and 86, all in the cranemobile, move out onto the flat, park near the paloverde tree that looks most likely to provide a semblance of shade, string the net around the tree, break out camp chairs, water jug and food, and make the best of a very sweaty situation.

"That day all hell broke loose." Now what does that mean? Now that the motorized migration of October 1995 is over, I can say that bad news, even exciting bad experiences, is far better than wondering and waiting for something to happen. I envision hell as some kind of prison, self imprisonment. Not intentional self imprisonment, just the result of careless misbehavior that leaves you damned, like a river is dammed, pooled up, waiting, unable to move on, waiting for who knows what and God knows when. For three days and two hours, we were damned to this kind of hell. And for those who sat in the "shade" of that paloverde "tree," Sonoran hell is the worst kind (a paloverde is a squat, deliquescent green-limbed shrub with sparse tiny leaves or none at all). Even 86 looked bored. Yes, this had turned into the sit-and-wait crane migration out of hell.

The afternoon wears on. The Air Force truck returns. No radio signals from the valley, so they chug up the mountain to Peeples Valley. Ben and I go to the Arrowhead Bar, about one mile from the paloverde camp and place a phone call. Maybe Cathy, my migration coordinator's wife, knows something.

Surprise! A Mr. Welch of Yarnell saw a big tame bird wearing jewelry out in the desert. He called the Arizona Game and Fish Department, who called the U.S. Fish and Wildlife Service in Albuquerque, who called Cathy. It's Miles, the leg dangler, they are discussing. We drop the phone and rush to Yarnell to find Mr. Welch.

Yarnell is small and we are intent, so before long we are discussing with Mr. Welch, the elder, how to locate Miles. Mr. Welch says it flew down and walked up to him: it was tame and friendly "just like a regular animal." He also says it cost him $4.65 to inform me about the crane. I break out my wallet, pay, and meet Tony, Mr. Welch the younger. He is thin, wiry, beardless, fortyish, eyes narrow-set and not parallel, energetic but friendly, busy sorting cantaloupes, and anxious to help. He selects two beauties for us, then says, "Follow me." It is my privilege to report an example of true Western hospitality: this guy dropped his work, used his gas money, and led us down the mountain from Yarnell, then across seven and a half miles of dirt-road desert toward Bagdad, to show us a bird that very likely had already long since flown away.

It was dusk when we turned off the dusty road, bumped across the wash, and lumbered up the hill to Tony's machines. And there, walking about in the headlights of the car was Miles. From that moment on, we all referred to Miles, so named because his voice reminded Curt of some rock star I had never heard of, as Miles-Tony. We exchanged appropriate goodbyes: "Thanks so much," "No problem, good luck," and drove away with Miles-Tony tucked under Ben's arm in the front seat of the Scout.

An hour after dark, we put Miles-Tony in 86's paloverde cage, and exchanged news with the crew. They had earlier picked up one radio signal west of Yarnell, but the battery in the receiver had died so they found a friendly face with an electrical outlet and put it on recharge. Ever since we lost our birds, I have been debating about sprinting home to get a second antenna and second receiver: this settles it. At the Arrowhead Bar, Ben and I call Cathy to meet us at the half way point, Casa Grande, and we start on a 300-mile evening jaunt.

Just as planned, Cathy is waiting by the ramp at the junction of Highway 387 and Interstate 10. She is more than a little upset: there's a weird guy wandering about in the darkness, so she's very relieved by our timely arrival. She has some other good news: crane 116, the comely favorite lost on 3 October, was seen flying north up I-17, then captured today south of Flagstaff. She is residing now with Christy Van Cleave, Arizona's most noted raptor rehabilator, in the sandstone capital of the West, Sedona.

It is 1:30 a.m. when Ben and I roll back into the paloverde camp with its four sleeping people and two cranes. We share the good news about 116 and drop into deep sleep.

Day 6: 7 October. The sun blasts over the cactus-strewn horizon too early and too hot. In this part of the world, every day feels like an ozone hole. Begrudgingly, I yield my hold on the far happier world of dreams. But, to the task: teams must be formed and sent out. First, Curt and Yoshi do a radio search far west toward Bagdad. Maybe Miles-Tony was not alone.

Brian and I go a short distance toward Bagdad to focus more closely around the spot where Miles-Tony was found. An aged pickup truck, rocking like a stage coach, lumbers toward us. Good information sometimes comes from very unlikely sources, so we wave him down. "Him" turns out to be them. A bedraggled, eagle-nosed rockhound missing his front, left, medial incisor sits at the wheel. He is accompanied by a very short, round-faced wife with grizzled hair equaling his own unkempt hemp pile. We ask. He answers, "Nope. Hain't seen no cranes, but last year a pair nested out east of Congress in the desert and before that, three pair were up on the mountain toward Bagdad." I sit there clutching the steering wheel trying to act pleasant while he reveals further absurdities. He pauses, his chin rises slightly, then a foul stream of well-salivated tobacco erupts for, I'd guess, 400 milliseconds through the hole created by the absence of his left incisor. Much of the dark venomous fluid runs down the door of his truck . . . a quick glance at the truck reveals that this hain't the first time he's missed terra firma with his brown spittle. Brian and I, too tickled to speak, mumble our thanks, then lumber away laughing loud and long. "Nope. Hain't seen no cranes."

After their Bagdad detour, Curt and Yoshi are to drive north along our migration route, listening to their scanning receiver all the way back to Flagstaff. Then they are to rush south, pick up 116 from Christy, and rejoin us at the paloverde camp. Ben and I, with the second receiver, radio search from the valley floor east of camp, then we return to camp and decide to search from the ridges of the Weaver Mountains.

First we ride the Scout back up the mountain to the scene of the crime. No cranes, no eagles. I break out my .22 and ask Ben to be all eyeballs while I shoot boulders scattered across the mountain slopes. I hoped to flush an eagle from a crane carcass and learn something. I shoot, eyeballs scan, echos fade, flies buzz, but we learn nothing. Hell must be something like this.

64

With news that 116, has also been found, we hope the nadir of our expedition is past. As Ben and I plod north along the route already searched in vain by Curt and Yoshi, we spot him. There at the road edge, unconcerned about the ten-day-trend in the stock market, about the war in Bosnia, about the recent bombing in Oklahoma, about the cranes of the world, is our bewhiskered bicyclist. So far we have learned nothing by stopping to ask the man on the street, so chances are in our favor. "Yea! I seen about six cranes go by, six it was, yesterday. They was all headed south. You guys are working for the CIA aren't you. I knowed it." Why bother to correct his count to eight cranes? Why bother to say, "No. FBI!" We leave him to his own distorted minuscule world and return to our own. I'm more than a little disappointed that this pedaling pilgrim had not worked out a formula for world peace.

To continue the search, Ben and I drive to the ridge tops and listen for beeps. Then at 2:30 p.m., we pick up a strong signal from the northeast. Ben runs cross country following the signal thinking it is from Peeples Valley. I drive around, meet him in a cow-clogged meadow, then we listen and drive north and east for fifteen miles. It seems to be coming from the ridge of the Bradshaw Mountains. As we rush on to Wilhoit trying to determine if the beeps are from below us to the southwest or above us to the northeast, our receiver dies. More dark thoughts. We retrace our steps back to Yarnell, arrange for a guy at the miner's supply store to recharge our receiver, speed down the mountain to the paloverde camp to trade Ben for Brian, who appears to have spent more than enough time under this shadeless tree. We zoom to Yarnell, discover that the kid running the miner's supply is untrustworthy (i.e., absent), impose upon our cantaloupe-vending friend, Tony, connect our receiver to Welch's rickety woodshed, tear north a few miles, note a dead coyote hanging from a fence, and at dusk rumble four-wheel-drive style to a hilltop viewpoint to enjoy the evening and wait until dawn brings recharged batteries and a new day.

Day 7: 8 October. Up early, we bounce down into Peeples Valley to retrieve our freshly recharged receiver, and at 7 a.m. from the Mountainaire Store, I call John Goodwin, our closest contact with the Arizona Game and Fish Department, and learn that three cranes are hanging out at the soccer field by the Coyote Springs Elementary School in Prescott Valley. Thank heaven for the wildlife enthusiasts of the world. From the band numbers, we know these are the same cranes we were radio tracking yesterday when our receiver died. We take time to alert our teams that we are headed for the soccer field, and call for a six-man rendezvous as soon as the team returns from Sedona.

By 8:30 a.m., two strangely clad, unbathed, unkempt craniacs sheepishly prowl around the soccer field at Coyote Springs. Our beeper says the cranes are very near. Yes! We see the three cranes: four kids are catching grasshoppers and feeding them to our cranes. It would be a little embarrassing to run off the kids and retrieve the cranes, so we back off a half mile, walk out into a field, squawk and flap our arms. The cranes are all heads up. They posture, then run and flap, lift off and glide down the hill to us. The kids stare our way, wonder what magical power accompanies these strangely clad earthlings, wonder what tale accompanies these wonderful birds, lose interest, and wander back to the soccer field.

I leave Brian with the cranes and speed to the rendezvous site. By 9:30 a.m., the whole crew arrives, cranemobile, Air Force truck, and all. Well, hallelujah! We have got six cranes, almost a flock, and there is a big temptation to resume the migration. A decision is needed: the Eisenhower principle finally proves useful. We are going to stay until we find our last three cranes. I call Dave Hunt, a pilot with the Arizona Game and Fish Department. He volunteers to try to set up a flight. We drive to Peeples Valley to call about the flight. At noon, David Hunt says the flight is on, "Meet us in Wickenburg in one hour and bring your own receiver."

The excitement was intangible. No matter what anyone tells you, excitement is always intangible. Further, it cannot be cut with a knife. Now we needed another decision, and we needed it fast. Who is flying and who is spending the afternoon in the Arizona heat? I think Ben should fly, as a reward for his selfless service. Ben is okay with not flying. I would like everyone to fly. Brian does not want to fly. I would like to fly. But Dave Hunt said two persons only, so I do the obvious: Curt and Yoshi spent much of their summer testing the radio telemetry equipment and much of their migration searching on the ground. They are to fly. They divest themselves of unneeded equipment and sprint away in the Air Force truck. The rest of us hole up with the cranemobile and the Scout under a box elder tree in a wash at the road edge, near Kirkland Junction. The highway bridge provides 100% canopy shade, the first we have had for three days. Four of us wait, doze, and slap flies.

We are planning and hoping that when the Game and Fish plane passes, it will tell us where to go to get our cranes. The afternoon wears on. Even up here at 4,100 feet, it is hot. At least we are not stuck in the paloverde hell camp. There is a buzzing in the sky. Heads up, we listen to our two-way radio. Curt calls down to us, "No signals yet." I urge them to just follow the route north. We wait. The aircraft disappears north. There is another, less distant, buzzing, more flies. The afternoon wears further on.

Finally at 3:30 p.m., we hear the distant drone of an aircraft engine, and Curt comes on again. "We've got a good fix on Meerta. She is at Garland Prairie!" We listen incredulously, Garland Prairie. We were expecting to wait six months to one year before we knew if the cranes could find their way back to the start of the route, and a single eagle attack, which until now has been viewed as a mega-disaster, causes Meerta, and who can say who else, to fly 80 miles, crow miles, right back to the start of the route. What good news. And whoa! Think about it: the three Coyote Springs cranes were 65 miles direct vector, on route to Camp Navajo. With this news, a joyous wave swept over us like a warm tsunami. Maybe you can cut excitement with a knife.

Okay, Plan A is for Curt and Yoshi to go to Garland Prairie as soon as possible, capture whoever is there, build a cage in the back of the Air Force truck using the welded wire corral we have been carrying, then meet us back at the paloverde camp tomorrow as early as possible. Matt thinks they should take the cranemobile. I decide no. Tomorrow, we will learn that Matt gives good advice.

That night at the paloverde camp we fall off to sleep with visions of sandhill cranes dancing in our heads. Curt and Yoshi are pushing hard to get to Garland Prairie before dark. In their haste to rush north, they forgot to take adequate sleeping gear for the nightly freezes at 7,000 feet. They badly need sleep, so they decide to spend the night in the shower room/dormitory on the military base at Camp Navajo. At hourly intervals all night long, an alarm goes off and morning finds them bleary-eyed but obligated to go on.

While the Air Force truck was racing to Flagstaff, I tried to borrow some electricity at the trailer park behind the Arrowhead Bar about one mile from camp. There I met Don, who owns the Arrowhead Bar and who agrees to recharge our receiver and two-way radios for free, but he would sure like to see our cranes fly by. I make plans to accommodate . . . bad idea.

Day 8: 9 October. The eighth day of the incredible motorized migration. Incredible is an ambiguous word. At 8:20, I call Cathy and she says Curt and Yoshi caught two cranes (not three, only two) at Garland Prairie and left Flagstaff at 7:20 a.m. I go to the paloverde camp elated that we are going to leave here today and never look at this spot again as long as we live.

Back at camp, we conduct a friendly debate over which cranes they have. Almost certainly Meerta, the Fair, for it was her radio that led them there. But who will be with her? Will it be Dennis, the Schizoid, everybody's least favorite bird? In the past when we moved our birds, this subordinate, paranoid crane took more time to capture than all the other cranes together. She is the only one who has figured out how to escape capture even after we lure her into the corral. She just jumps over. On the other hand, it could be Baka, the Reformed. Once a renegade, Baka now is liked by all.

We sit around with sweaty elbows on sticky knees, rubbing our hands, writing notes, waiting and wondering. The temperature creeps ever upward. Life seems to be one long doze. But then we realize we are not alone. A middle-aged, pot-bellied, shaggy-headed miner strolls toward our camp. His two dogs rush on ahead of him. I cannot allow these over-friendly canines to rush up to the crane pen, so I shout, "Call off the dogs." He very calmly retorts that they are not going to hurt anyone, but I shout again, so he calls them to him. Actually, I am kind of amazed that he did not get riled at my very gruff response, no matter how justified it was. I walk to him to explain, to quell any anger. He is perfectly calm. His attitude reminds me of a karate expert confronted with novice ruffians. I get the feeling he is a little too under control for everything to be all right. After a few moments conversation, he turns to walk away, and I see the reason for his self assuredness. There, tucked into his pants, wedged between his bulging right buttock and his blue jeans, and revealed by his undersized T-shirt, is a machine pistol with an 8-inch clip conspicuously attached. Suddenly I am very glad I did not throw a rock at his dogs.

While four of us sit here enjoying the denizens of the desert, watching the sun rise higher into the ozone-depleted sky, taking turns pretending we are in the shade, Curt and Yoshi, now at Flagstaff, are not having a good time. After a long night of frequent interruptions, they got an early start south, but while speeding along on the divided highway, their makeshift pen caught an updraft and launched from the back of the pickup. With it went Meerta: she was flipped into the air, but landed without injury as the pen tumbled to a halt. As for Dennis, she just stood there, confused and penless in the back of the speeding pickup.

The guys return the pen to the truck, and this time fasten it more securely in place. Cautiously, Yoshi and Curt continued on for another thirty miles. Then Meerta tried to fly, was caught in the turbulent air behind the cab, got blasted into the pen convolutions, and hung there. After this mishap, Curt rode the rest of the trip in the pickup bed trying to calm his charges.

And so our eagle-inflicted ordeal winds down. Curt and Yoshi are rushing south with two birds to join the six in our paloverde pen. We are less than five miles into the Sonoran Desert, fearful that it may be too hot for our cranes to cross, but nonetheless anxious to begin the effort.

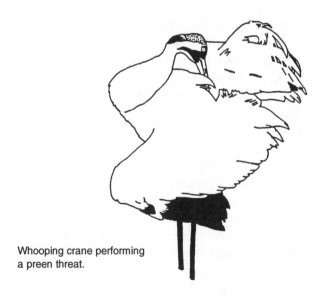

Whooping crane performing
a preen threat.

69

Chapter 8

South to Sonora

It is 11 a.m., and the Air Force truck hasn't arrived. If we do not leave soon, it will be too hot to fly the cranes and we will waste another day. It is definitely a good thing I was not advising Eisenhower at Normandy. We leave messages at the Arrowhead Bar so Curt and Yoshi can find us and tell Don, "The cranes are coming by at noon." Bad idea. By 11:59, we have warmed up the vehicles (the people have been warm since 8 a.m.), begin rolling forward, and have the cranes striding along behind. We squawk, wave, and gun it, sending dust into the midday heat. The cranes squawk and wave in turn, and we are off.

First we race two miles west to the main road, then turn south, hoping the cranes will not overtake us. We make the turn, but the cranes pass us. It is neck and neck as we approach the Arrowhead Bar. Uh! Oh! About thirty people are standing in front of the bar, and several of the guys have on red baseball caps. Despite our frantic waving and squawking, our six lovely cranes brake and glide to a beautiful landing fifteen feet from the bar patrons. We turn around, drive back to the flock, smile at the nice people, line up the cranemobile in front of the cranes, and then wait until the crowd loses interest and returns to booze or pool or darts or whatever you do in a bar at midday.

We start squawking, and the cranes start gawking and walk a few steps as the cranemobile pulls away, but they have had it. It is 90°+F, and we want them to fly! They would rather sit on a bar stool. This is very embarrassing. I signal for the cranemobile to back up, then get ready to pull away again on my signal. I sweep around behind the cranes in my Scout and gun the engine. The cranes leap out of the way, suddenly discover they are following the cranemobile, and we are back on the road again.

We have not gone a mile before every bird is panting again. We glide along at 30 mph. The birds are looking bad. You can read their little avian minds, "Want water, want shade." After four miles, we come suddenly upon the northernmost limits of the Northern Ranch Trailer Park, a gravel-covered island in a sparsely clad creosote ocean. The temptation is too great. The drooling cranes plop ungracefully between the new motor homes and their aged owners. What to do? We join them.

We move the cranemobile in close to provide shade, fill the water bucket, and spray the birds down. Soon the over-thick saliva disappears from their bills. However, their panting continues longer than I would have liked. It is simply too hot to be doing this, but what is our alternative? After a half hour at the overheated Northern Ranch, a less-than-polite attendant tells us what to do . . . "these facilities are for human patrons." So be it.

We load our bucket and squirt bottle, call our feathered friends to attention, attempt to run them down with the Scout, and are back on the road again. We pull out at 1:17 p.m.: the birds are already panting and it is getting still hotter. Four miles later is the turn off to the Merv Griffin Ranch. Merv knows nothing about our coming, but our cranes can go no further. We veer left, skid to a halt, jump out, and gather our overheated birds into Merv's entry, away from the highway. We move one car fifty feet off the road, leave the other one conspicuously perched in case the Air Force truck comes by, and settle down into the pretended shade of a paloverde. "Nice trip." "Yeh." "Need a bath." "Naw, I can wait." "Be nice to get something cold." "Yeh!" "Yeh!" "Yeh!"

The profundity of our locution is interrupted by the hoped-for, but unexpected, arrival of two very cheerful, but overtaxed craniacs and two somewhat worse-for-the-wear cranes. We quickly off-load Meerta and Dennis. The former looks okay, but the latter suffered extensive primary wear on the wire of the well-ventilated pen. We go to work spraying and sleeking her damaged feathers. After we are done, I pronounce my judgement: Dennis will be unable to fly with the group.

At the present temperature, the group cannot fly with or without Dennis. At 5 p.m., it is beginning to cool off. We are only 135 miles down our 400-mile route. We decide to chance it.

Two miles ahead, our road joins Highway 193. It is divided, fast, but not too busy. We move the vehicles into position, ready the vests, helmets, and stop signs, then call to the birds. It is time for heads up. No traffic coming forward. No traffic behind. We charge out onto the pavement, and amazingly the birds join us. The lead car, my Scout, sprints to the "Y" intersection ahead, and I bark a command into my two-way radio, "It's okay: blast on through."

When approaching a complex intersection not offering a clear view, the word blast seems strangely inappropriate, but Matt responds by speeding around the corner without losing the seven birds flying strongly, if not happily, in tow. Dennis rides in the back with Brian, and excitedly calls to her flock mates. Curt and Yoshi also blast on through, then Ben and I jump in the Scout and rush to catch up.

In only two and a half miles, we are to turn south toward the Vulture Mountains, so we in the Scout sprint ahead to find and point out the turn-off. When approaching the turn, the cranemobile creeps ahead of the flock, lumbers around the turn, then continues south through the suburbs of Wickenburg. We are all hoping we can get out of town before the cranes get overheated and drop into a neighborhood. The only real obstacle before the Vulture Mountains is a long hill topped by an intersection controlled by a stop light. Both the Air Force truck and the Scout zoom ahead to open the intersection. The light is favorable, and we scramble for our cars as the cranemobile rolls through with our little flock of aerial athletes churning air trying to top the hill.

As I roll down the hill, the intersection disappears in my rear view mirror. All I see is a flock of cranes topping the rise, then flaring and dropping down out of sight. It looks as though they've landed in the intersection.

Three normally sluggish cars execute high speed turns and convergence on a busy suburban intersection. Some of us jump out and sprint to assist the cranes, others tend the cars. It is 5:32 p.m. The sun will very soon set; the drivers heading west are looking at feathered silhouettes against an over bright golden orb. Somewhere in celestial realms, someone is smiling on us, our cranes, and our project. When we arrive, all of our birds are placidly pecking at stones and whatnots in an empty lot on the far side of a very busy intersection. We rather sheepishly, but thankfully, call in the cranemobile, load the birds, and drive south out of town.

A few miles later and nine minutes after sunset, we find a wide spot in the road, unload all our cranes but Dennis, and rush off, hoping to make a few miles before dark. This is actually the very best time to pass through the Vulture Mountains. Golden eagles are diurnal, not crepuscular. From the many days I have watched goldens from blinds near their nests, I have noted that they consistently go to roost early and try to avoid moving in fading light. I suspect their telescopic vision is adapted for bright light, not shadow. Nevertheless, I lead our little procession over the hills and beneath the beetling crags with a shell-cracker loaded shotgun out the driver's window. Ben rides beside me, .22 at the ready. If anybody squawks "eagle" on the two-way radio, I plan to put some lead in the air and discuss intentions later.

Without incident, we chug over the pass through the Vultures. As we leave the eagle-bearing cliffs in the rear view mirror, we descend a long, slow decline into the gathering darkness. We shunt left into the first available turnout and call down our cranes for the night. Although we rush, all is done with complete order: Matt and Yoshi care for the birds while the rest of us make a quick pen selection and toss our net over the thorny, leafless scraggle that has been given the melodic name, ocotillo (o-co-tea-yo). Next we spread the net east to a paloverde, and west to another shrub. Within fifteen minutes, the pen is up and filled. Wood is quickly gathered, Yoshi's cot is up, the water is boiling, and we settle in. Though we are missing Baka, we have eight cranes: life is good.

After dinner, the moon rises: it is nearly full and bright enough for persons under forty to hunt snakes. We opt for bed. Our campfire wanes: the remaining coals slowly disappear into a bed of fluffy, gray ashes. I hear a flurry of scuffling noises thirty feet from my sleeping mat. A kit fox trots into view. Lacking fear and without hesitation, it saunters to the fire, scoops up a chicken bone, and crunches noisily. I dare not move or say a word for fear of spoiling the scene before me, but how can I not let my comrades enjoy this moment also. I blend my voice into the night sounds, "Heyyy guyyys! Heyyy, looook. Seeee the foooxx." The word passes through the drowsy crowd, and soon six beady eyes from the ground, two beady eyes from the cot, and four beady eyes from the roof of the cranemobile are watching the strangely non-beady eyes of the fox as it scurries here and there about camp finding morsels where only a sharp nose could. Once it skipped to within ten feet of my head. Yet its visage was so bright, its comportment so coordinated and precise, that I felt not a trace of fear for rabies. Who could fear a six-pound fox with teeth all smaller than the pinky talon of an eagle!

In five minutes he is gone, his tummy half-full. We lie there, our memory banks raging full speed, playing the scene over and over. Never to forget: never forget. The cranes gurgle in quiet conversation. They have had a big day, especially Dennis and Meerta. They, we, and perhaps the fox, have all lain down some long-term memories this day.

Day 9: 10 October. There is no problem rising early when you are sleeping ten feet away from eight cranes. Anxious calls preface the dawn. We are loaded and ready to fly south before the green flash crosses the horizon. Actually, I am red-green colorblind, so I can only enjoy the green flash in my imagination.

At 6:47 a.m., we squawk and flap out into the lead. All eight birds take off beautifully. Even Dennis with the scruffy primaries is allowed to fly. We have a great start and high hopes for many miles before the desert heat stops us. Very soon, Curt, in the following car, says he is missing a crane. "Dennis must have dropped out." Every head tilts toward the two-way radios. I pause. My brain does not pause. I think, how come I have to make all the tough decisions? Oh yeah, that's right, I am the "principal investigator."

"Curt we've got to keep going. Please drop back, give it a quick search, catch Dennis if you can, and race to catch up. We will need you at the crossings." "Copy. We are on our way." These guys are great. The team is great. I never worked with a better group. They let me make mistakes without second guessing me. I reciprocate as best my Type A personality allows.

The road is paved. There is not another car for miles. The cranes are cruising along at 100 feet with only Miles-Tony gaping. The morning sun turns their silver-gray wings to pink and orange. The next hour and a half are destined to be the most enjoyable of the trip. Curt and Yoshi soon appear in the rear view mirror. "Sorry, didn't hear a beep." "Thanks for trying, who knows, maybe she'll show up." We take turns driving in following position where we can photograph the birds. I try for a shot of the little flock with the towering crags of the Palo Verde Hills as a backdrop. Most of this flight is through some great saguaro cactus habitat. We and Kodak make the most of it.

I am a competitor, not by choice but by compulsion. When we began this migration, I knew that Kent Clegg (rancher, farmer, biologist, and pilot who would begin his own ultralight-led crane migration as soon as our trek was over) had once led tame cranes on a 38-mile flight behind a pickup truck, just to see how far they would go. It seems to me that it is fully appropriate that our truck-led migration have at least one flight longer than Kent's.

From the Vulture Mountains to the Gila River (where we, by decision, must stop to familiarize our cranes with this riparian area for future migrations) is 48.2 miles. Could the cranes, would the cranes, make it the whole way without a stop? Would the desert heat allow it? Would the sharp turns and traffic make the attempt prudent? There are twenty-four sets of powerlines along this leg of the route, most of them very near the end where our tired cranes will be less able to avoid them. Would it be wise to risk our little flock?

The miles slip away. One, two, three sets of powerlines, a backroad intersection, then sixteen miles of open desert before a stop sign. Then in two miles, we cross Interstate 10. The birds are keen on the adventure, the crew is trained. We are doing it. The chatter on the two-way radios is decidedly upbeat. The first stop sign is nothing: no traffic and no need to impersonate a highway crew. The Interstate crossing is not even a ghost of a problem. We go over the long ramp, speed unabated. Perhaps no one on the busy highway below even notices anything out of the ordinary as fourteen wings flash overhead. In the next one and a half miles, we have five sets of powerlines and a stop sign. The birds are high enough, and the lead car squawks to the cranemobile, "Road's open. Go for it." Matt does not even slow down.

Now for the tricky part. We have a stop sign at a "Y" intersection with powerlines before and after, then powerlines, a railroad crossing, another intersection, and ten sets of lines before we are on the home stretch. With the birds flying high and the Air Force truck and the Scout taking turns at being the lead car, Matt maneuvers all without even elevating his heart rate. For me at the metaphorical helm, an elevated heart rate goes with the job, but today all seems in our favor and I enjoy the trip as much as the craniacs, as much as the cranes.

At forty-six miles, we must make a sharp right turn and enter traffic on Highway 80 south. Highway 80 is a busy, two-way link between I-10 and I-8. The Scout is in the lead. As the cranemobile approaches, I try to coordinate an entry without stopping. "Matt, slow a bit now, then gun it and pull in after the semi. I'll stop the other cars." There is lots of traffic and high tension even without powerlines.

Matt makes the turn, but loses too much momentum, and as he lumbers forward, slowly gaining speed, the cranes swing wide left but pull in behind him. A huge, white semi also pulls in behind him, and now the trio (the cranemobile, semi, and cranes) slowly accelerates south, crossing the long, low bridge over the Gila River. The semi driver is all eyeballs, wondering at the flags, at Brian in the cranemobile, at the big birds swarming about him like bees over a newly opened flower. Will he let Matt slow down to make the 90-degree left turn onto the Gila River mudflat?

Ben and I are standing by the lead car on the mud flat, calling and waving to the cranes. Matt slows to turn, the semi closes in, close enough for Brian to jump onto his bumper. Brian forgoes the opportunity. The cranes veer left toward us by the river, leaving Matt to sort it out with the truck. The cranemobile bounces down off the highway. We have done it! The cranes have done it! They have flown 48.2 miles, achieving a new world record, and only Miles-Tony is panting.

It is only 8:15 a.m. and not yet too hot to fly again, but I decide to give the birds at least a full hour to rest, feed, water and explore the shores, hoping they will form long-term memories for future migrations.

As the cranes and craniacs poke around reveling in the morning's successes (forget losing Dennis: everyone was very tired of Dennis anyway), I look at the maps and envision the route ahead. We are nine days into the migration, a migration that I thought would take five days, and we are just now at the half way point. Eagle Mountain looms three miles to the west. The radio says, "unseasonably hot weather will continue in Phoenix and the surrounding areas." What should we do?

We stand by the edge of the Gila River. Weeks earlier I failed to find a 35-mph road allowing us to continue southwest. So we truck the birds in a long loop from the Gila River, north to Buckeye (a prosperous farming community of 4,000), then south out of town to the northern edge of Rainbow Valley (one of those places where water is mined in an attempt to turn the Sonoran Desert into a cotton patch).

It is 10:20 a.m., and the birds stand near the road edge panting even before the first flap. How far can they go in this heat? If we go, where will we find shade? The trucks start up: the birds are not convinced. I pull the Scout around behind and rush at the cranes. They flee: the cranemobile lurches forward. We are doing it, but one glance at the panting birds rowing along barely above the road, and we all know that this cannot last long. At six and a half miles, two birds momentarily touch down, then race to catch up. In 200 yards they do it again. For a half mile, my mind races searching for a solution. Suddenly the answer looms ahead: a dozen eucalyptus trees stand like 60-foot sundials at the road edge. Shade! We grind to a halt: the cranes gladly join us and the shadows.

For the first half hour, all our attention is focused on our overheated birds. Every one of them has a terrible case of dry mouth. Long gossamer strings of saliva dangle from each bill. Quickly we supply water, and methodically we spray each overheated leg. Soon the cranes are cooled down and in the shade. The craniacs also relax, some sitting, some lying, but all in the shade. The long slender shadows creep slowly eastward, delineating the minutes until sunset. We, gruids and hominids, creep along with them. Doze a half hour, move east, doze, move, doze, move.

The monotony is broken by our discovery that there is a red-tailed hawk nest in one of the eucalyptus trees. A prairie falcon perches on a distant snag, then flaps briskly through camp, calling everyone to attention. Matt has a bright idea: we are not too far from cool drinks and air conditioning in Buckeye. The craniacs go in shifts until all are refreshed.

I have a different mission. Seventeen miles to the southwest, Ben and I have an appointment with Tom Horton, outdoor writer for *The Baltimore Sun*. *The Sun* has prevailed upon my supervisor, George Gee, to allow Tom to accompany us. I long ago learned the wisdom of keeping my name out of the press, but Tom seemed like a nice enough guy, so reluctantly I agreed, but for one day only. In my openly stated opinion, nothing could be more dangerous to the project than to have the world know what we are doing. My idea: tell the world after we are done, not before. Ben and I bounce our way south along the El Paso Natural Gas pipeline to our rendezvous with fame. Ben is to return Tom's rental car to the airport in Tucson, then rejoin us after Tom leaves.

That evening, Tom meets the guys, the cranes, and the vehicles. He is doing a story so he is full of questions. "How old is the Scout?" "1976," I answer. "How old is the cranemobile?" "No one knows. We can't read the plaque on the door."

One half hour before sunset, all is being readied for a sprint south. The sun's domination of the day has lessened. The cranes seem okay. We are going to see how many miles we can eat up. At 5:35 p.m., we lift off. The cranes are doing fine, but they are staying right at deck level in the dust behind the cranemobile. How long can they pump like windmills while they are sucking dust like vacuum cleaners? After eight and a half miles, I call a halt. It is still too hot to fly. We water the birds, watch the sunset through a cactus strewn horizon, and then get ready for another try.

At sixteen minutes after sunset, we are back on the road. The birds are still flying through the billowing dust, but at least they do not look over heated. After two and a half miles we turn onto the gas line right-of-way. It is not really a road, and there are lots of small washes to cross, so Matt must speed across the 20 mph flats at 40 mph, then rumble through the 10 mph washes at 25 mph. From what I can see, Matt has finally convinced Brian to hold on so he does not catapult out in front of the cranes.

We are bobbing along, doing at least twice the reasonable speed along this roadless pipeline: the overtaxed springs on my Scout keep me informed of recent developments on the Richter scale. We are trying to keep an eye on the cranes overhead, when suddenly Tom learns why he prefers to count the cranes from within the safety of the cab. One crane lets fly with a cloaca full of excrement: it hits dead square on the windshield. Although there is no need to stop suddenly and defecate the window, the splat is nonetheless huge. Errant fragments are strewn across all quarters of the glass. Who says doing science can't be fun?

The incident was not wasted on Tom. More note taking, and sure enough, a few months later, the dirty trick by our crane of large cloaca became a "baseball size feces" and immortalized in *The Baltimore Sun*.

A dusty darkness settles over our procession. I am in the following car: every 20 seconds Tom and I try to count the flapping objects in the ever darkening dust cloud. "Seven, yep." "Sure?" "Yep, seven." Half a minute later, "Seven?" "Yea . . . maybe seven . . . I think six." "Sure?" Silence. "I think there's only six." "Be sure." "Six, the leg dangler is gone." I gun the Scout, spin a circle left, jump from the car, tear off a mesquite limb and throw it in the track to mark the spot. Then we zoom on. I contact the other cars, now far ahead, "We think Miles dropped out. Let's pull right and camp."

It is too dark to be sure of anything, but when the cranemobile slides to a halt, only six cranes land. Miles-Tony is lost. Two guys stay with the six remaining cranes and set up camp. The rest of us grab our flashlights, pile into the Air Force pickup bed and head back northwest. My plan is for Curt to drop people off at quarter mile intervals until all are searching, then we all walk northwest calling, while Curt waits in the truck. After a half hour, he is to return southeast and retrieve all, one by one. I am the first one to jump out, and I start searching just south of where I think we lost Miles-Tony. I can see the tail lights of the truck as they bob away growing ever smaller.

Quiet settles. I listen, then take a few steps. I call my crane gargle call, listen, walk, gargle. After only 200 yards, I hear a distant "seeep," pause, "seeep." Great! I have found her. In the time interval since we first lost Dennis a few days ago, Miles-Tony has assumed Dennis' role of schizoid, paranoid, subordinate. She hangs out near the other cranes, but is terrified of close contact. She also will not allow people to approach. She is even more upset as I close in under cover of darkness. What to do? It is a battle of wits. A 16-cc neural nodule of mostly cerebellum (great for flight and balance) squares off against 1,600 cc of mostly cerebrum (great for cunning and pursuit). In the winking beam of my flashlight, I herd Miles-Tony into a wolfberry bush. She stumbles, pokes and pushes: I grab her bustle, then her wing. No contest.

The Air Force truck reassembles all and we bounce southeast to camp. For tonight at least, we have seven birds.

Day 10: 11 October. Through the night, electrons rearrange themselves in the nicad batteries in two-way radios being recharged in the elementary school in Mobile, Arizona, population five (the kids come from the environs, not the town). The nice lady swore she would meet me at 5:30 a.m. to allow me to retrieve my radios. She shows up at 6, flustered, apologetic, and helpful. A dog got into her trash bin and scattered its contents to the hot Sonoran winds. I reckon the trash would have still been there after school was over, and it would have been mummified, less stinky, shrunken, and lighter. I keep my thoughts to myself.

It is 6:29 a.m., and we have flown into action: the cranes are peeping along behind us. In a mile, we bounce onto a dirt road and whiz past Mobile in less time than it takes to spell it. Then our entourage ambles out onto the paved road paralleling the Southern Pacific Railroad. We speed east into the rising sun. The dogs in the trash gave us a later-than-hoped-for start, but for now, all is well. Like the cadence of a metronome, the tenths of miles tick away. Always in the dark recesses of my mind there has been the recollection that two of our cranes have already fallen: when will it happen again?

Approaching the little burg called Maricopa, we take a cutoff to pass around the north side of the town. There is a stop sign ahead: we all know about it: it should be no problem. I am riding tail. On the horizon ahead, I see many cars zooming north and south at right angles to our route of travel. I hope the Air Force truck can open the intersection. I am too far back to see the Air Force pickup, but I see the cranemobile lumber through. As we approach, I see a guy in an orange vest and helmet holding a stop sign. Great . . . craniacs control the intersection, but why is there a string of five cars stopped directly ahead in my lane? I assume it's craniac power at work, swing heavily left, and sprint past the pooled-up cars. As the Scout climbs up onto the crossroad with fast traffic approaching left and right, I look into the face of a craniac I have never seen before. It is not just that his eyes are much wider than more familiar faces. With a dull thud, the thought clanks into the forefront of my mind. This isn't my guy and he hasn't stopped the oncoming traffic. I punch the accelerator, trying not to reveal my innermost thoughts, hoping that Tom Horton, professional writer, does not understand how close he came to an early appointment with Rafael, the Angel of Death.

Three miles later, we make the sharp right turn at the corner of a pecan orchard. A beautiful coyote saunters along about to enter the cool of the grove. Back home, my eagle is hungry: I grind to a halt. Tom later reported in print that before we even stopped, a cold cylinder of steel lay across his chest and a quick report was heard. The coyote loped off under the dense canopy. My own recollections of the incident are clouded by time and are discretionarily vague. I do recall slogging through the mud far into the grove to see if the coyote was injured, recall concluding that it was fine, and recall, that same day, removing the telescope from my rifle and later giving it away because of this and similar near misses. As I sped away with clenched teeth, trying to catch up with our little team, I reflect how a single coyote could feed Lothvar, my lovely eagle, for nearly a month.

When we rejoin the team, they are parked barely off the pavement, nervously assessing the traffic and trying to keep the cranes off the highway. It is now 7:31 a.m., hot and getting hotter. We have got to get away from this shadeless spot. Police officers sit in two cars a half mile ahead. What are they thinking? Do they like what they see? Both cars start up and approach. I look nonchalant and urge everyone to look nonchalant. The officers drive west toward six weirdly-dressed and determinedly nonchalant people, seven cranes, and a cranemobile with flags unfurled. Surely this is the most suspicious thing they have ever seen in their lives. I comment to Tom that in Arizona it is not illegal to migrate cranes down the road, not yet. From the cops there is not the slightest glimmer of alarm, not a hint of recognition. They just drive west and disappear into shimmering mirages.

Fearing that these cops may, upon reflection, come back to query us, I call for a quick departure. We line up the cars for takeoff: the cranes look hot. They are ignoring our waving and squawking. Then another not-so-tiny miracle happens. A huge steel behemoth rumbles in from the west along the Southern Pacific tracks. The panic-stricken birds fly toward mother cranemobile. We are back on the road again.

Not for long. After only two miles, the migration sputters to an overheated halt. We cannot wait until dusk out in the open between the pavement and the railroad tracks. A decision is made. We load the birds and drive fourteen miles to the far side of Casa Grande, then unload them in an area of citrus orchards and open fields.

Our birds are hot: we are hot: the roads are hotter still. Picacho Reservoir, the next major migration stopover, is only twelve miles away. I decide we will try one more flight. The trucks line up. The birds look uninterested. The trucks move out, craniacs squawking and flapping. The birds are heads up, but only three move forward. Then two follow, but the others are not budging.

81

Then it happened: three guys who had been working in a nearby citrus grove were also watching us tend our birds. Unbelievable as it may sound, they correctly interpreted the situation, assessed our need, and sprang into action. Even though the leader was a white-haired, fifty-five year old with a lot of extra weight aboard, he and his crew charged the last two cranes, flushed them, and then stood watching us disappear east. Back on the road again.

Within a mile, our vehicles climb a manmade hill and we are once again looking down at I-10. The cranes are hot, but still with us. Two more miles east, a strange thing begins to happen. First, two birds drop back and, for a second, light on the road, then they rush to catch up. Then three cranes drop out of sight into a canal that parallels the road. Oh, they are still flying. I can see their wing tips now and again, but they are more or less flying subterranean.

Next, four cranes land in the road. Curt in the lead car barks, "There is a pickup coming." Twelve beady eyes squint at the pickup. I yell, "Matt cut off the pickup." I grab the wheel, gun the Scout, and spray dirt in a 180° arc. As I charge back to flush the cranes from the roadway, Matt and Brian jump out of the cranemobile waving and shouting, trying to stop the pickup truck. The driver is a woman. She has her kids with her. All she sees is two weirdly clad, dirty, bearded guys trying to steal her babies, her truck, and her . . . whatever. She doesn't stop, she doesn't slow down, she guns it: Brian and Matt dive out of the way as she fishtails past the cranemobile, heading for our little beauties. Fortunately, I get there first and the cranes are safely flushed aside.

We gather our birds: Miles-Tony had dropped out at a dwelling 200 yards earlier. This schizo bird again tries to evade capture, but once again grey matter prevails over white. With all seven on board, we drive, tail-between-legs, the remaining seven miles to Picacho Reservoir. Our little flock, cranes and humans, burrow into the jungle-like tangle of tamarisk bushes for shade and await cooler temperatures.

At the phone booth ten miles away, I learn from Cathy that Baka, missing since the second eagle attack, showed up on the Tonto Apache Reservation 65 miles northeast of the attack site. We need some decisions. I decide. One team must take the cranemobile and go for Baka. I will drive Tom, our journalist, to catch his airplane from Tucson. The cranes need a rest, so we will rest them here today, all of tomorrow, and be ready to fly out on the 13th—Friday the 13th!

None of us need a rest more than do the cranes. All of us need a bath. Tom and I head toward Tucson. Tom has had so many experiences in one 24-hour period that he offers to write a book on the project. I try to sound optimistic about his book idea, think about all the quasi-legal things he has seen, and hope that he gets busy on other projects. At my home in Oracle, Tom and I bathe, rest, and I arrange for Ben to rejoin me on the migration late tomorrow night. The craniacs at Picacho Reservoir take turns visiting places with warm water and cold air.

On the evening of the 12th, I rejoin the squad at Picacho Reservoir and learn that the evening's entertainment featured Yoshi's dance after stepping on a scorpion. As a result, most of the guys are sleeping either in or on the cranemobile. As I set out my sleeping gear beneath the dense tamarisk bushes, I listen to the wailing of a distant coyote and the baying of a not-so-distant bloodhound. All the cranes are loose, just hanging around the camp. One crane decides to outdo Yoshi in providing entertainment: It wanders into the firepit, burns its toe, trumpets an alarm, and rockets into the night sky. All the other cranes, equally alarmed (if uncertain why), join the branded crane, and zoom off into the moonless night. Some of the guys are fast asleep, but in an instant five of us are on our feet and thinking at near record speeds of how to undo the damage. In the very dark sky, the cranes, unable to see well, do not know where to land. They fly about, peeping loudly. We all commence Gawow-calling and Brood-calling, and in an instant, I get Brian and myself busy illuminating the road with flashlights. Joe, used to greater expenditures of funds than either Brian or me, calmly walks over and turns on the headlights of a car. Four birds line up parallel with the runway, lock landing gear down, and glide onto the illuminated road. The remainder, too frightened to land, circle overhead again and again, then finally touch down at various places in the darkness.

Five of us scamper about trying to find the cranes. Occasionally we hear a peep far off in the night. Joe and Brian find two within a half mile of camp: both are in a very tall cotton patch. One of these is actually suspended two feet from the ground in the dense cotton. After these two are retrieved, another crane comes from somewhere and lands on our landing strip. Later Yoshi and I drag our bodies through a half mile of tamarisk brush and capture 50 in the beam of our flashlights. Not sure that I can follow the same tunnel-like path with a crane in my arms, we pick a new route and learn that it is twice as long, but at least we can walk upright.

Walking with 50 in my arms, I suddenly feel the warm, wet slurry of crane excrement rushing over my right hand (an occupational hazard of those who transport cranes using the Patuxent "football carry"). Because I'm slumping over trying to miss tree limbs overhead, the excreta sprays and plops onto my right foot. No water handy, so we just tromp on through the night. By the time we get back to camp, the goo has dried on my foot. A short time later, all the cranes are safely recovered, so we take time for ourselves and rinse off our hands as best we can. It is midnight: we reposition our mosquito nets, then drift quickly into chase-that-crane REM sleep.

Day 12: 13 October. Up very early, I discover yet another reason for not wearing sandals. Last night I forgot to wash my foot before crawling into my sleeping bag. Not to worry, the crane stuff comes off easily enough and whatever flaked off in my bag will eventually shake out.

By sunrise on 13 October, we have loaded the cranes and transported them to the main north-south road three miles from Picacho Reservoir. At 6:39 a.m., we take off — this time with eight birds in tow. The cool air invigorates the birds, and we make good progress. With the cranes at 300 feet, we pass through the town of Picacho. We are proceeding southeast, parallel with the railroad tracks, when Ben and I, in the lead car, spot a potential problem. In a half mile, our road crosses the railroad tracks. There is a train ahead of us on the tracks, and it is heading toward our crossing. The train is very long and is going very slow. If we do not get the whole squad across the tracks, we will lose the morning flight and be stuck again in the open desert.

I gun the Scout and grab for the two-way radio. "Matt, Curt. Listen carefully. Go fast now! You see that train up ahead. We have got to beat it across the tracks or we are dead in the water (figuratively speaking, of course)." Ben and I pass the train, lumber up onto the tracks, and sit there broadside. We keep the engine running. Our guys are racing toward us. We do not intend to be run over, we are just hoping that the train slows enough for the migration to pass. Our worries were all for naught. We bounce down off the tracks in time for the cranemobile to lumber over, then the Air Force truck. The train is still fifty yards away.

The birds are looking great and making greater time. Then in two miles, one hits a powerline, falls to the ground, bounds back up, and rejoins the flock. A leg dangles slightly and temporarily. Then in another mile, a second crane flutters at a wire. Did it hit? We do not know for sure.

The flock is overheating now. Since we crossed the railroad track, we have been driving a frontage road, with I-10 running parallel immediately to our right. The birds drift right and are flying over traffic. Four of the birds get alarmed by the thick, fast traffic below and veer to the south 200 yards. Miles-Tony with leg askew is with them. They drop lower and then cut back north, trying to regroup with us and the other cranes. They get frightened by the big trucks, veer, scatter, and regroup without Miles-Tony. The Air Force pickup falls back to stay with Miles-Tony. The migration proceeds another half mile. Miles-Tony flies across the highway, but lands in the desert to the north. This bird is making life very complicated.

We slow down and pass a jogger, a fifty-year-old, sweat-drenched male testing the limits of his as-yet-undiagnosed aneurism. The guy has no blue and white anorak, and no red baseball cap, but the cranes prefer the company (or the speed) of this total stranger to us who have fed, cared for, and sacrificed for them since infancy. Seven cranes land at his side: the guy, absorbed in an endorphin-induced runner's euphoria, glances blankly at the big birds and runs on. The cranes are left behind. Then they fly forward and rejoin him, again and again. We stand watching, mildly entertained, knowing this incident will provide one very big long-term memory for this pilgrim. Finally, the fellow jogs up to us and delivers our cranes. As he sweeps by I ask, "Having a nice day?" "Oh, yeah," he exclaims. To humor us, Brian queries, "You're not going to the Buenos Aires Refuge are you?"

We gather the seven and go off in quest of the one. With radio telemetry, we determine Miles-Tony's general location, then four of us hike off through the scrub trying to find her. We lose fifty minutes of our precious morning flight time rounding up the scoundrel (can females ever be scoundrels?). We decide that Miles-Tony rides in the cranemobile on the next leg of the journey.

At 8:27 a.m., it is already getting hot as we push on with seven cranes in pursuit. Our path continues southeast parallel to I-10, then after seventeen more miles, we cross the freeway. This time the cranemobile has to go under the Interstate, a maneuver that is a little more confusing for the birds. We have planned our approach so the cranemobile spurts ahead of the birds, passes under the freeway, then reappears on the other side, to lure the cranes over the freeway. All goes perfectly. This was a very important crossing because the birds are tired and panting and if we had given them any excuse they could have landed on the . . . well, things could have been . . . "not good."

Only one mile from the Interstate, the cranes are getting lower, hotter, and are looking for a place to land. We approach the town of Marana. In the lead car, I see five black kids hanging out by a pickup truck: my alarm goes off. Either I hide these kids, or the cranes will land by them, in town. I slow as I pass, then blare into their surprised faces, "Hide. Quick, hide. There's a flock of pterodactyls coming." Just as soon as the words escaped my lips, I realized that most people would run out in the open and pay big money to see a flock of winged dinosaurs. The kids interrupt their methodical consumption of ice cream treats to stare blankly in my direction. Plan B, I gun it, pull a hundred yards ahead, slam on the brakes, then Ben and I leap out and wave and squawk with all our might and lure the pterodactyls past the kids. Then we jump into the Scout and lead the cranes out of town before they land.

It is 9:19 a.m., it is hot, and it is going to get a lot hotter. We give up on any more flights this morning. We have a right to be more than pleased at the thirty-four miles the birds have flown today. We quickly load the cranes in with Miles-Tony, and sprint three miles to the Arizona Sonora Desert Museum. We avoid all the "visitors parking" signs and enter the museum compound. We crowd the cranemobile into the partial shade of their warehouse, then scout around trying to find someone to officialize our invasion. Everyone is friendly and cooperative, so we soon have permission. We check on the birds at regular intervals and occasionally drench the roof making the whole crane box into an evaporative cooler. The guys tour the museum (actually it is a zoo) while I escape for a few hours.

After about four hours, we all rendezvous at Ben Trahan's house in southwest Tucson. Toward evening, we move the cranemobile back onto the route. At 5:36 p.m., eight cranes are standing in a vacant lot surrounded by a tall saguaro forest. Three vehicles pull away squawking, whistling, and waving. Every crane stands at attention: every crane begins to walk slowly toward us, but not one launches. I spin the Scout around in the road, whiz past the cranes, spin around again, and charge toward the ambivalent cranes. All eight burst into flight.

Excitement has replaced the pursed lips and clenched teeth that carried us over most of the route. We are now only about fifty miles from the conclusion of our journey. Tomorrow is an open house at the Buenos Aires National Wildlife Refuge, and I have promised to introduce the cranes, discuss the project, and perhaps fly our birds for the assembled masses. We must get within striking distance of the refuge tonight.

The cranes cover seven miles without a hitch. Then leg-dangler, Miles-Tony, drops back and disappears near a small housing area in the mesquite barrens. I decide that we must not further retard our progress by halting to search for Miles-Tony. We proceed another five miles before our flock trails off behind us and alights. Very quickly, we round up our birds and truck them to a suitable camping spot five miles further toward our destination. As the crew is busy penning the birds and making camp, Ben and I drive back hoping to find Miles-Tony. Until it is fully dark, we scour the area where we saw her drop down below the mesquite canopy. We interview several residents of the small housing complex. They promise to call if she shows up.

Back at camp, everyone is optimistic about, and anxious for, our arrival tomorrow morning. We enjoy a quiet evening cooking over a mesquite and ironwood fire with chunks of the lattice-like skeleton of cholla cactus tossed in for the bright light it emits. The cranes purr quietly in their pen at the perimeter of the lighted ring surrounding the fire.

The conversation turns to Miles-Tony and her chances of surviving the night with coyotes all around. Although this, the least cooperative of our remaining cranes, has slowed us down, frequently earned our ire, and consistently aggravates us when it is time to capture cranes, she is still our responsibility and we are all concerned for her. In the context of this emphatic consensus, I make another bad decision. I agree to postpone our departure tomorrow morning until we search for our juvenile delinquent, Miles-Tony.

Day 13: 14 October. Dawn comes and with the first brightening of the eastern horizon, Curt and Yoshi rush off with radiotelemetry equipment to search for Miles-Tony. Four more craniacs pack gear, disentangle the net from yet another paloverde tree, and get everything ready for a final push.

The sun violates the eastern horizon. With the first white-hot rays, the chill of the night evaporates. I would prefer to be on the road by now, but not to worry. We are at a higher elevation now so there is not the same need to rush to get the cranes underway before it gets hot. Hour 6:00 comes and goes without the Air Force pickup; 6:30 and no Curt and no Yoshi; 7:00 and still we wait. How did Eisenhower ever do it? I absolutely hate this sick, sinking feeling as our window of opportunity slowly, unremittingly closes. By 7:20, the Air Force truck arrives sans Miles-Tony, but with apologies for their lateness. I am not the sort to lie to the guys and smile away my inner turmoil. With visible tension, we spring into action, and at 7:28, we are on our way south.

It is not hot and the birds look very good on the wing. They pump along only sixty feet above the ground. Each stroke looks strong and each flap eats up more of the 37.5 miles between the refuge and us. Baboquivari Peak looms above the horizon. For me it is a beacon welcoming me back to the refuge, to the place I once called home.

No problems arise as we tick off fourteen miles, then 94 hits a powerline, drops down a dozen feet, dangles her leg but keeps flapping and regains the altitude of the flock. The group is now panting and looking for a place to land. They make four more miles before I call a halt at the road edge. It is 8:17, we have covered 20.1 miles, and it is only 17.4 miles to the end of our trip. The birds are panting just as pathetically as when in the low desert. How could this be happening? Our migration is fizzling this close to success. Dark thoughts creep into my head. Only one thing to do: make the best of a bad situation and go on. But going on, under these circumstances, means pushing the birds when rest is needed. After a twenty-six-minute rest, we call our little flock back to attention and lead them on south. They begin panting almost immediately, but it is nearing 9:00 and we must push on to our appointment.

The birds are hot, flying only a wing-spread from the ground, one nearly hits a road sign. They push on only because we fall back and call to them. We coordinate our vehicles so the cranemobile is ahead, but not too far, then we in the Scout, in following position, drop back so we are within twenty feet of the churning wings. The birds call to us pleading for a break. I feel selfish pushing them on, submitting to peer pressure, trying to meet an appointment, trying to avoid going to our 10:00 appointment to report on a fizzled migration. How much better it would be to complete the migration, then cheerfully report our successes. I look at those pleading, trusting cranes working "their hearts out," trying to keep up with us. I hate myself as I call at them, urging them on.

A large brick and wood sign is seen ahead on the left. We have done it! We are now on the Buenos Aires National Wildlife Refuge. But it is still sixteen miles to the headquarters and the ramshackle quail pen we have renovated for our cranes. Now it's thirteen miles, then only seven remain. How long can the birds hold out? I fear the cranes will die of heat prostration even if we get them there. The humane thing to do is stop, wisdom dictates stop, obviously we should stop. I talk to the cranes and talk via two-way radio to the craniacs urging all to go on. "Don't stop, maintain position, we are all but there."

Five miles, four, then three remain. 86 is my favorite, the only bird that stayed with us to the bottom of the Weaver Mountains. He has flown every time and every mile any other bird has flown. Panting and calling, 86 veers left and drops out. We all grimace as we watch him move off, then land. It is three miles to the refuge headquarters. I radio, "Keep going, keep in formation." I hate myself. I realize that my decision is motivated, not by my concern for the birds or for science, but by my concern that I not look stupid at some insignificant gathering of hominids three miles and forty minutes in my future.

One mile from the headquarters, we make a sharp left into the front gate. Curt, in the lead car, has pulled ahead and is waiting for us, camera in hand, compelled by some inner force to document our arrival. In the rush, he is parked in the slide zone for the cranemobile's turn. The cranemobile must not slow lest the cranes drop out, so Matt rushes on, clanks over the cattleguard, skids around the corner toward the Air Force truck, toward Curt half out of the window, camera in hand. I am driving the following car and see it all. Dark thoughts spew from deep recesses in my still unperfected brain. I like, respect, and appreciate these guys so much that I suppress the darkness, crush the thoughts

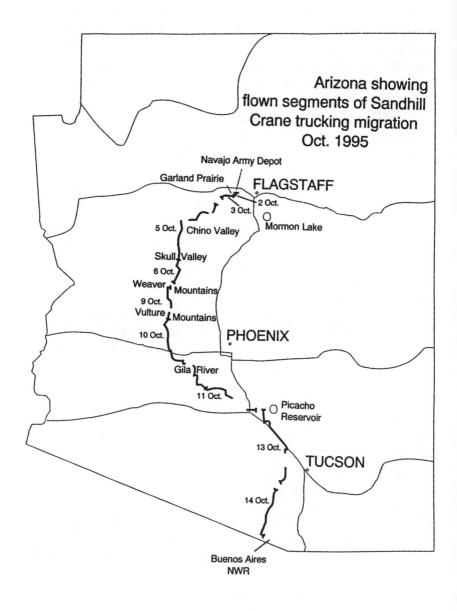

Arizona showing flown segments of Sandhill Crane trucking migration Oct. 1995

Fig. 2

that would only injure, but bark into the two-way radio a command, "Curt, go back and get 86." My words would deny his participation in the last mile of our odyssey, would disallow his seeing the cranes cross the finish line and alight in a sudden flurry of wings, miss the excitement of success. I quickly correct myself, "Curt, stay with us and we'll go back after 86 later."

Now we have two following cars. We rush on through the light haze of red-brown dust cast skyward by the cranemobile. We see six little athletes struggling to stay aloft. One half mile ahead lies the beautifully picturesque adobe and stucco buildings, former headquarters of the Victorio Land and Cattle Company, now headquarters of the Buenos Aires National Wildlife Refuge, the road takes a sharp left turn. A decision is needed. I decide that this turn will be the terminus of the world's first motorized crane migration, the world's first truck-led migration for any species.

At 9:15 a.m., six sleek but exhausted cranes plop down unceremoniously as the cranemobile grinds to a halt at a non-picturesque, dusty intersection. Two more cars pull in behind the cranemobile. I am full of anxiety. Everyone springs into action trying to keep our beauties alive: a bucket quickly appears for drinking water and a spray bottle to cool legs. We begin to wind down. We have arrived. We are glad, relieved, and emotionally exhausted. I am half distraught at the loss of 86, half angry at the near collision at the front gate. The sweetness of our success is much diluted by the turmoil of the last ten minutes. I glance toward the refuge headquarters. A small group of watchers is trailing off to other curiosities, after observing our arrival. We need some decisions. I decide. I will go to the headquarters, assure people of our arrival, and ascertain the schedule. Three craniacs will help the six cranes recover while Curt and Yoshi go for 86. Hominid heart rates return to 60 bpm: gruid to 70.

The Air Force truck quickly recovers 86, and within two days, Miles-Tony, found on the roof of a garage, swells our ranks to eight. By October 28, Dennis, lost in the Vulture Mountains, was found. By some, by many miracles; some large, some small, nine birds are still alive.

Within an hour of our arrival, seven cranes are safely penned and the craniacs and thirty other persons crowd into the undersized conference room at the refuge. Using a few slides and lots of emphatic ges-

91

ticulations, I revealed the process of training cranes, and many of the happenings along the migration. The craniacs packed together in the back of the room are clearly excited by my presentation, but as I drone on, I realized that our experiences of the last thirteen days are so far removed from the realm of the audience that, interested though they are, and attentive though they try to be, our migration is as foreign and irrelevant to them as the genocide now underway in Bosnia, the masses dying in Rwanda, the perennial fear gripping Belfast.

Once the open house has ended and the craniacs have devoured a considerable, but not offensive, portion of the refreshments really intended for the voting public, we retire from the headquarters building, conduct a safety inspection of our crane pen, and then rendezvous for an expedition portrait at the massive sign by the refuge entrance. Baboquivari Peak looms in the background, presiding over this event just as it loomed and presided over the arrival of cranes in the Pleistocene. I am wearing the official expedition T-shirt, a gift from the craniacs. On the front are drawings of a feather and a truck tread track, on the back a quotation from a meeting long ago and far away . . . "Basically, we have no idea what we're doing."

The End of the Beginning.

Chapter 9

The First Winter

With our safe arrival at the Buenos Aires Refuge, our experiment was just beginning. The tension and trauma of the migration were behind us and it was time to relax, celebrate, and settle into a routine for the winter ahead. Very soon after our arrival, most of our craniacs dispersed. But one or two stayed on for a few weeks to get the birds settled in, to work on data, and to release some of our survivors into a wild flock on the Gila River.

Thanks to our hosts at the Refuge, housing was made available. This was in the form of a room or two in a not-too-bad trailer house. Matt Shawkey kindly stayed with our cranes for the first week or so. On the evening of 20th October, I moved Matt into the trailer. While Matt checked out the closet, I inspected the bathroom. There I noted an adult female black widow spider nicely webbed into the shower stall. Remembering Matt's aversion to scorpions when a month ago he visited my home and remembering that rather than risk a midnight scorpion attack in my house, he slept that night in the truck, and not wanting to risk Matt's early departure due to arachniphobia, I decided some fast action was needed. In an instant, I spotted a plastic bag on the dresser and quickly pulled this over my hand. My hand gloved in plastic, I plucked the spider from her web. In a rush, with Matt just in the next room, I inverted the bag over the spider, crammed the partially closed bag into an empty peanut butter jar (unfortunately lidless), and stuffed the whole of it (spider, bag, and jar) down the neck of my shirt

Whooping crane performing ruffle-bow threat.

and against my tummy. For the next five minutes, I tried desperately to act cheerful until I could excuse myself, get out of doors, and divest myself of the jar and its loathsome contents lolling about my naval. I remember thirty years earlier, on a dare, releasing a four-foot-long, striped racer inside my shirt. When the snake began to slither across my chest and back, the "willies" were almost uncontrollable. Some of you can imagine the overwhelming, flesh-crawling revulsion during those moments prior to extracting the peanut butter jar and its venomous contents. Fortunately, the spider was still in the bag. It now safely floats in alcohol along with 100-plus scorpions (captured in and around my house).

Matt never learned of the spider, so he quickly settled in at the government trailer. And just as quickly we had the cranes settled in. We repaired the holes in the former quail pen and trimmed the most dangerous limbs on the thorny mesquite shrubs in the pen. Our cranes immediately learned to go around the few remaining thorns and no eye injuries resulted.

Once every week or so all through the winter, after my helpers left, I would make a trip to the Refuge to check on the birds and release them for a flight. Each time, 86 and his buddies met me at the gate ready to rush out and lift off. Only Miles-Tony hung back, avoiding not only me but the other cranes as well.

Wanting all the cranes to participate, I had a minor logistical problem trying to get the last crane out of the pen before the others had flown. Usually this was accomplished by lunging into the pen and thereby intimidating the friendly cranes, then rushing around behind Miles-Tony and forcing her to flee through the gate so she wasn't left behind.

These flights were always dramatic even though they normally lasted only a few minutes. First, the birds would fly directly away for a quarter to half a mile. I would call "Gawowuuu Gawowuu" until they turned and circled back. Then they would pass overhead again and again until all would dangle legs and settle to earth at our feet or perhaps 100 yards from where they first began.

When the flight was over, the "fun" began . . . trying to get Miles-Tony back into the pen. To herd the others in first was a mistake. Not only did Miles not want to be confined with the more aggressive cranes, she would more earnestly avoid capture herself if she had just seen us coerce the others into the pen. Part of the solution was to always have a second crane herder handy. Together we would herd the flock past the pen, then when Miles-Tony, always in the rear, was near the gate, we would quickly wheel about forcing her against the wire, then through the gate. Patience is essential in working with "trained" animals, but to be honest, this process of recapturing Miles-Tony after each flight was sometimes so frustrating and so time-consuming that thoughts of an early demise for Miles-Tony kept creeping into my consciousness. Once I just gave up and left her outside, then called the Refuge asking them to pen her the next day after she grew lonely . . . and cooperative.

So, for most trips I took along a volunteer, first, to enjoy the flight, and second, to earn his fare by helping me herd Miles-Tony. It was always a great treat for me to see the surprise, wonder, and elation on the faces of those who witnessed these flights. First came the surprise when I opened the gate and the cranes burst into flight. Next came alarm as the entire flock energetically flapped off into the distance. Then came the wonder as the big birds made a long, slow turn bringing them back our way, sweeping low overhead with the wind whistling through their wings. Finally, when the birds alighted at our feet, my guests had the pleasure of mingling with the birds that had, just a few moments earlier, seemed likely to disappear into the sky. I often promoted this mingling by distributing a handful of crane pellets to each guest.

Of all these experiences, the one that pleased me the most was introducing the cranes to the children of my comrade-in-bird-studies, Chuck LaRue. With the sleeves of their adult-sized costumes dragging on the ground or waving wing-like above their shoulders, eight-year-old Catherine and five-year-old Charlie scurried out to meet the cranes. The cranes were taller than the kids, so I was a little concerned that the big, unintimidated males would peck one of the miniature humans. However, the kids were almost as quick as the birds. I long ago formulated the axiom, "Life is too precious to be wasted being perfectly safe," so I did not deny little red-headed Charlie and tow-headed Catherine the crane experience of a lifetime. I did, however, hover protectively to make sure no harm came.

And so the winter fled. By February, wild cranes in the valleys far to the east and west of the Refuge were soaring each day into the afternoon sky, testing the thermals, and preparing for their hormone-driven odyssey, anxious to begin again . . . north to the breeding grounds. Would our cranes also go?

Shetigan, an ethnic Kazakh living in extreme western Mongolia, with his byerkoot (golden eagle). For thousands of years such birds have been trained to hunt hares, foxes and even wolves. Our work training cranes was inspired by this knowledge.

Sandhill crane chick, newly hatched and ready for training.

Yoshi encouraging a sandhill colt toward the cranemobile.

Curt with our crane colts exploring the marsh at Camp Navajo.

Our first efforts to train cranes to follow a truck were to test various radio harnesses.

Crossing the oak savanna south to Skull Valley.

Nemesis of the 1995 migration, a golden eagle on the attack.

The cranes trail past Vulture Peak by evening light.

Rest stop at Picacho Peak. Less than 100 miles yet to go. Matt (left) and Brian with the cranes.

A pigeon joins our little flock on their longest flight, 48.2 miles.

Photo: Joseph Duff

Only one day left to go. Our tired and over heated cranes follow along only 15 feet from the highway. Expedition vehicles used flashing lights for safety.   *Photo: Joseph Duf*

Baboquivari Peak towers over the Buenos Aires National Wildlife Refuge where our 1995 cranes wintered. Pronghorn in foreground.

Our cranes at Mormon Lake with San Francisco peaks in the distance.

After a world-record flight, 86 rests in the cooling waters of the Gila River.

Right: Our cranes probe the muddy shallows of Chongo Tank.

Above: Two prairie falcons were trained to fly with an ultralight aircraft.

Photo: Ken Franklin

Left: John McNeely with the red-tailed hawk he trained to fly with his hang glider.

Photo: John McNeely

Opposite top: Swans were trained to follow a motorboat.

Photo: William Carrick

Opposite bottom: Bill Lishman and Joe Duff repeatedly led geese south, the first ever motorized migrations.

Photo: Duff and Lishman

Above: Sandhill cranes were trained to fly behind a pickup truck so we could test various radio harnesses.

Right: We modified our army ambulance; one cot became the ramp. Our 1995 team in uniform.

Below: Training cranes to use the ramp in 1994, our pilot year.

Sandhill crane chick with a stuffed crane head (used to teach chicks to feed) and a whole stuffed crane (used to supply heat to the chicks).

Our 1996 costumes resemble gray ghosts.

Brian took the most difficult chore, riding in the back, luring the birds along.

Cranes in hot pursuit of the cranemobile.

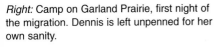

Brian and two friends work on the expedition log at Camp Navajo.

Right: Camp on Garland Prairie, first night of the migration. Dennis is left unpenned for her own sanity.

Cranes and craniacs rest for a few moments before proceeding through the ponderosa pine forest west of Camp Navajo.

Five cranes decide to rejoin our migration on Garland Prairie.

Opposite top: After Brian and I launched the birds on the east rim of Hell Canyon, the other craniacs call them west across the gorge.

Opposite bottom: Cranes passing through powerlines near Drake, Arizona. Here we lost beautiful 40.

Opposite top: Golden eagle in a predatory stoop. Golden eagle attacks were a constant threat.

Below: After a 40-mile circuit, the cranes hop out of the cranemobile ready to begin another leg south.

For three days, we took turns waiting and wondering in the "shade" of this paloverde "tree."

Our cranes relax in the shallow water of the Gila River.

Long shadows of the eucalyptus trees shade us and our overheated cranes.

Right: 320 confined to a pant leg but content after her long journey.

Below: Our cranes enjoying shade at the Antelope Hills Golf Course.

Miles-Tony and 86 wheel over Chongo Tank. Baboquivari Peak towers in the distance.

Marsh at the edge of Mormon Lake, beautiful and teaming with life during the summer.

On the last day of the migration, the cranes wing their way south past the National Observatory.

Our cranes move into the nearly frozen marsh at Mormon Lake.

Sam supervises the release of our four survivors at Chongo Tank.

Chapter 10

The Spring Migration That Never Came

B aboquivari Peak, Arizona's glacier-less Matterhorn, that towering silent sentinel, has presided over Altar Valley affairs for millennia. Visible from seventy miles and more, it dominates the skyline. At 7,730 feet above sea level (pre-global warming standard), it is more than a thousand feet higher than anything within forty miles, and higher than anything between it and the Sea of Cortez. It stood there when the masked bobwhite was abundant and when the last masked bobwhite disappeared from Arizona nearly a century ago, and it witnessed the return of the quail to Arizona following the establishment of the Buenos Aires National Wildlife Refuge in 1985.

The Altar Valley was probably never important to cranes, but a few cranes likely wintered there at the scattered natural cienegas (spring-fed marshes) that once dotted the valley. The winter of 1995–1996 was probably the first time in a century that cranes wintered in the Valley, and these did so only because they were in a pen.

Thirty thousand cranes winter in Arizona, but generally only in three areas: one in the Sulfur Springs Valley far to the east, one along the Colorado River north of Yuma, and the third along the Gila River far to the west of the Altar Valley. Come late February, they begin to trickle north. By late March, they are all gone. So through February, each time I released the cranes for exercise, I watched our survivors very carefully to see if they had any interest in going anywhere. There was no sign of pre-migratory restlessness, so I decided to transport them a few miles from their pen and release them three days each week.

To get ready for these weekly releases, I had bands to change, radios to replace, and other miscellany. It is not much fun wrestling cranes alone, so I cast about for a low-paid assistant. Fortunately for me, Ben Trahan had a son with lots of traffic tickets and no desire to do jail time. There is often an alternative to high fines and jail: it's called community service. Now Chongo Tank, our chosen release pond, is many miles from anything that could be considered a community, but my government letterhead was convincing proof that this project was on the up-and-up. Roark was temporarily out of work, and camping with cranes sounded like more fun than collecting trash at the roadside, so I had myself a volunteer. We made everything legal by having Roark fill out the official volunteer agreement that promises a life on easy street if you can somehow accidentally injure yourself while serving your country.

10 a.m., 5 March 1996, Operation Stick-in-the-Mud begins. I arrive at the Trahan household: tall, lanky Roark appears. With a two-foot-long, blond pony tail and developing beard, he looks the part of a 1960's hippie. He swings his gear into the rear of my Scout, and we are on our way to adventure. By 12:30, we are at the Refuge ready to exercise the cranes. They pace excitedly at the gate as we position ourselves for their exit. The gate opens: all eight birds march out onto the gravel lane. At first they peep along behind us with fluffed feathers and heads low. Roark and I are in our crane uniforms so we can join in the fun. We move slowly into the group, call Gawoww!, raise our arms and begin running and flapping into the wind. All eight birds run and flap and launch. They describe long, low circles in the warm spring sky: three laggards begin to drop down. The other five make one more quarter-mile loop and soon all eight are purring and peeping around our feet. Only three radios are working well, so we have radios to change before the cranes are ready for their big migration. We herd all but one into the pen, change water, add food, then begin our examinations.

It is always best to begin with the schizo bird, so we grab Miles-Tony. She looks good and her radio is okay. She is very plump and, at 4.1 kg (9 pounds), is a hefty little lady. Next comes 86 and he gets a new satellite transmitter. At 6.1 kg (13 pounds 6 ounces), he is our biggest bird. Next comes 229, then 116. This little female is going to take some work. She has a compound fracture of the right toe on the right foot. A bone protrudes about a quarter of an inch and the toe is hooked strongly to the right. Roark settles into our routine very quickly. His big hands and arms gently cradle 116 as I clean the wound, extract the protruding bone, splint, salve, and bandage. We hope the Baytril (antibiotic) I inject will reduce the swelling so she does not miss the big migration.

As we are working on 116, my buddy 86 is poking about next to the medicine kit and radio transmitter supply box. I glance his way and see him snap up a pop-rivet, complete with its two-inch nail. In a flash it is gone, down the gullet! I wonder what his stomach is going to think of that! Hardware disease is well known among cattlemen, and it has recently become the bane of crane colonies as well. Once a crane named Lothvar Junior (yes, he was incubated and hatched by my eagle) snatched a gold earring from Dee Thompson, one of our head chick-mamas, and no one saw it again until the x-ray was developed. Objects made of inert metals like gold are no problem unless they have a sharp point, and after a few weeks erosion in the gizzard, they are small and getting smaller. Nails on the other hand can be troublesome. Our worries for 86, as described in the following chapters, could very easily stem from this incident.

One of the bad things about handling cranes is that you often cause more problems than you solve. We have fixed 116's toes, but in the process, 86 has a nail in his gizzard. Next up, 10 slashes at us with her feet and puts a one-inch gash into the thick scaly skin of her right ankle and another gash on her right foot. When it is all over, we have handled all eight cranes, caused two injuries, and fed a nail to my favorite bird.

We decide it is too late to safely release the birds this evening, so we pen our birds, then go to Chongo Tank, inspect its shorelines and shallows, and decide that at half an acre, it is good enough. That evening, we return to the refuge headquarters to work on our radio bands and charge the battery on the radio receiver. Somehow, it did not occur to me that the employees would go home at 4:30 and lock up the shop. Here we are standing around, cursing our luck (better known as bad planning), when I discover that the three-inch blade of my pocket knife has somehow jimmied the lock. The heavy metal door swings decisively aside . . . bingo! We are back in business. Quickly we drill one-eighth-inch pop-rivet holes in the bands. While I am busy doing this, Roark finds a long extension cord and runs it outside so we can charge our receiver where we can retrieve it early tomorrow, without messing with the lock.

Long after dark, we drop by to see our birds. They each stand on one leg, quietly snoozing in their pen. Roark and I are not keen on camping in a crane pen, so we return to Chongo Tank, in the dark, without our birds.

Early morning, 6 March 1996, we lie snug in our sleeping bags waiting until the first rays of the sun strike the face of Baboquivari Peak. Up in a rush, we have birds to get ready for release and a radio receiver to recover before someone takes notice. Back at the shop, Danny and Frank are already at work painting the inside of a water tank to go in Brown Canyon. Both are pretending to escape the cancer-causing fumes by wearing gas masks. So while Roark retrieves our receiver and surreptitiously stows the extension cord, I have this very strange conversation.

Danny: "Mmmmmm pmmmmmm?"

I can tell by the inflection of the last "mmm" that Danny has just emitted a sentence in the form known as "the third intonation contour." In other words, it was a question. I decide to humor him.

Me: "Yes, we stayed last night at Chongo Tank." Danny: "Mmmmmm pmmmmm bwarree?" Me: "Yes, it looks like it is charged okay." Danny: "Mmmpu rummm pmmr." Me: "Thanks, I think so." Danny: "Mmmmmmmm." Me: "Sorry."

I have no idea what I'd confessed to doing, and Danny probably had no idea why I was confessing, but it just slipped out. No repercussions followed, so it could not have been too upsetting, even if refuge personnel did conclude that we had broken into the shop the previous night.

Now it is time to attach new transmitters, so our second bout of crane handling begins. Our first bird is 10. He immediately flails and the inner (killer) talon on one foot slashes the other. Again, I play veterinarian. One quick stitch holds the foot injury closed, a quick wrap with gauze and tape, then 3 cc of Baytril and he is ready for his new transmitter. Soon he is released and back into the pen. Our next victim is Baka. We complete our work, but as Roark goes to release him, he also flails and the damage this time is far worse than for 10. He slashes his own neck. The three-quarter-inch gash is bleeding profusely. Birds, with their very high body temperatures, are great at fighting off infections and this wound stays closed on its own, sort of, so we just wait and watch until the blood flow stanches on its own. 116 still has a swollen foot, so we give her an injection and allow her to march back into the pen.

We have enough injured birds that I decide it is time to call a real veterinarian, Dr. Glenn Olsen, Patuxent's finest crane clinician. We discuss possibilities, then decide that only five of the eight birds should be released. The other three must wait in their pen but probably can go in a week.

Roark and I load the five healthiest cranes, including 86 who has only minor injuries, into the cranemobile and fifteen minutes later we are at the turn off to Chongo Tank. For five minutes, we lumber along the dirt road, trying to avoid hurting the birds as they jostle about. We open the rear doors of the cranemobile, and cautiously, hesitantly, the big birds peer out. Then, one by one, they whoosh down to the ground and make for the water. The first two splash into the pond, providing a powerful lure to draw the reluctant one from the cranemobile.

We move the cranemobile out of sight below the bank of the pond, and once the five are fully engaged splashing and bathing, we slip away ourselves. Once out of sight, we quickly doff our crane costumes but wrap these around two bushes, just in case our birds fly and need a costumed bush to lure them down.

Aware that the area is near saturation with coyotes, we feel much like a mother who has just left her toddlers with an ex-con baby sitter. We zoom back to refuge headquarters to get my International Scout. A half hour later, we are back with both vehicles. We don our costumes and check on our feathered charges. All five are quietly peeping and rattling to one another as they probe the shallows at the west end of the pond. We drive the cranemobile back up onto the bank and turn it sideways to act as a shade and windbreak, then settle in for our crane watch.

Now I am a professional bird behaviorist and my first hour watching a novel species of bird is pure fascination, but by the end of the second hour, it is time to insert toothpicks between the upper and lower eyelids. Roark and I have the task of babysitting our birds for the rest of today, sleeping by them tonight, and watching them until the end of their morning activity period tomorrow. The birds are going to wander some, and we have to be attentive enough to intercept coyote and eagle attacks until our neophytes become predator-wise.

So, first things first, out comes the shotgun. It is loaded with a shell cracker, and I lean it against the cranemobile near Roark. Next, I place my old Model 61, Winchester, pump action, .22 rifle next to me. Out come the camp chairs and all the arts and crafts tools and materials necessary to keep us busy while we are "incarcerated" with the cranes. Roark is young and energetic, so he begins hauling in logs and limbs of mesquite trees for a fire tonight. The cranes work their way upstream where the water is very shallow and the brush grows close to the shore. Aware of the great risk of predators, most of my concern is related to the cranes being unconcerned as they approach dense cover, so Roark and I amble past the cranes and herd them back toward the open pond. Deep down, I feel the uneasiness, the mild anxiety borne of experience, that our birds are very vulnerable if danger comes from the brushy quarter.

Roark has a "secret reason" for wanting to do community service with me. I am a flint knapper. Now I am not even close to being a great flint knapper, but I have made about a thousand stone tools, mostly arrowheads, and I enjoy both knapping and teaching others. So, I begin with the obsidian, flint, antler tines, hammer stones, and leather. I have taught knapping to a few dozen people, mostly Boy Scouts, and I can recognize a good student. Most kids watch half heartedly for a minute, then want to try it themselves. Roark is a good student. He watches for a half hour as I demonstrate pressure flaking and then go to percussion flaking and notching. Now he is ready to try it himself. So here we sit: cranes probing quietly along the shore, Roark and I sitting quietly snapping rocks with bones (antlers are bone), and all the while my ears, nose, and eyes are evaluating the risk of attack. Toward evening, the cranes work their way upstream again, and I get that nervous, uncomfortable feeling that all is not well. I stop my work and glare, closely examining each snakeweed and desert broom. Then I see a slight movement as a sand-colored coyote creeps toward the cranes. In a flash, I rise and chamber a shell. The coyote senses danger and bolts for tall cover as two lead projectiles whiz past his posterior.

An educated live coyote is more useful to our cranes than a dead one ever could be, so I let him escape. My plan is to teach the local coyotes that Chongo Tank is now off limits, then it is up to the local pack to exclude interlopers. If we killed the locals, uneducated immigrants would quickly replace them and the process would continue as long as we killed those we have educated.

We too have learned something. The local coyotes are brave enough to approach even in daylight, even when two humans are near. Roark and I move into Phase II of our coyote education program. We march to the brushy end of the pond and at fifty-foot intervals, urinate on the bushes. Canines have a special ability to put just the right amount of urine on each bush, tire, and fire hydrant. Not being canines, we make two or three trips that evening scenting the bushes around our pond. We walk out, scent, then return with a load of firewood, spend another hour breaking rocks, then make another trip. By dusk, we have a week's supply of fuel, a fragrant ring around the pond, and a growing collection of stone tools. It is a brisk, chilly day so, long before dark, we have a radiant fire ready for our soup cans.

At dusk, the cranes trail into camp, glare bug-eyed at the fire, peck at a few shiny objects, then, as if honor bound, they march, one-behind-the-other, out into the shallows, thirty feet from shore. Instinct seems to lure them offshore, but once there, curiosity lures them back to the fire. When near shore, Roark and I simultaneously rush at them with arms thrashing and throats blaring. Our strategy, before dark, is to rush at them. After dark, we crawl into our sleeping bags to thwart the night breeze, but before doing so, we tear the six-foot-long flower stalks off some yucca plants and use these to splash water at our birds to keep them out of camp.

Being a world class sleeper, I did not know until the next morning that four times during the night, Roark had risen and driven the birds back into the water. At dawn, we fight off another crane invasion, then as we lay in our bags waiting for the warmth of the sun, I write up the happenings of the previous day.

On 6 March, at Chongo Tank, three species of flycatchers entertain us with their quiet calls: the black phoebe (Arizona's indicator of standing water), the vermillion flycatcher (or Blood of the Bull, as our Mexican friends know him), and the Say's phoebe of timid voice.

Before the ashes are cold from breakfast, four of our cranes wander to the nether reaches of the pond, then all of a sudden they burst into flight but quickly alight. I rush over and fire a round into the desert just in case Mr. Coyote is listening.

The morning goes quietly. After breakfast, we dry our gear and pack for our departure. I have been watching our birds, trying to read their thumb-sized minds . . . do they have any interest in migrating? I have about decided that they feel no urge, when two of the cranes posture, call, then run into flight. They circle low over camp calling. Again and again they fly by until they have made about ten passes. Finally, they land and rejoin the group. I estimate they flew two to four miles in this bout. Maybe, just maybe, they do feel nature's call.

By 10:30, the morning activity period is passed, and the birds are resting, so we load the five cranes and haul them back to the headquarters. Before leaving headquarters, we inject two of our sickies with more Baytril and note that 86 has another weeping sore. Blood is running down his leg from an old injury. By 11:30, we have penned our birds, stowed the cranemobile, and are on our way to Tucson. So much for migration attempt number one.

Only four days later, we try again. The intervening time was not wasted. We have gleaned some coyote chunks from a roadkill and a few more from Lothvar's freezer. I also bring along a lynx hide and a plan on how to use it.

By 4 p.m., we have evaluated the sickies and decided to take all eight to Chongo Tank. The release goes smoothly, and as they busy themselves probing the shallows, Roark and I dangle seven chunks of coyote from the bushes around Chongo Tank. The local coyotes may be slightly lured in by the scent of strange coyotes, but if they are anything like humans, they are going to be repulsed by the knowledge that the interlopers are very dead. Chongo Tank is not a safe place for predators.

After awhile, five of our birds get excited, call, posture, and take off. They call as they circle overhead, but with three cranes, two Moms (us), and the cranemobile on the ground, no migration begins.

At about 6 p.m., seven of the cranes move to the west end of the pond. This is the danger zone, so we decide it is time for lynx lesson number one. Roark stuffs the lynx hide under his costume, disappears into the brush while still dressed as a crane mama. Then he ditches the cap and anorak, drapes the lynx over his back, balances the head on his own mane, and creeps slowly toward the cranes. I watch intently to record the interactions. Soon the cranes detect a shaggy mammal in the bushes, and as Roark rises slowly out of the brush, all seven lift their heads high and watch intently. Their contact calls change into a nervous burrup, and they march energetically away. After only a few paces, their quiet calls change into loud alarm trumpets, and they burst into flight. They circle a few times, give Mr. Lynx an aerial reconnaissance, then land near camp. For the next half hour, they nervously watch: Mr. Lynx is very much on their gruine minds.

The previous week we had our hands full fighting off hourly crane invasions of our camp, so we do two things to avoid a repeat. First, we encircle most of the camp with our stiff welded-wire crane corral. Next, to ward off nighttime attacks, Roark and I cut a dozen staves which I plant in a semicircle in the water between our camp and the crane roost. I have brought along a 4' x 60' net which will hang from the staves once it is dark. For now, the net lies furled, under water. At dusk, all eight move into the water; we keep them there with an occasional hoot, lunge, or slap at the water. I also try flinging flaming desert broom at them, but this frightens them entirely away from the roost, so that is a bad idea. When it is dark enough, I wade out into the frigid water and hook the top of the net loosely onto the staves. The idea is that in the night, if the cranes decide to raid camp, they will pool up behind the net barrier so we can sleep better and so they learn to stay offshore all night long.

In the campfire light, I see one crane go around the net: I scoop up mesquite coals with my army shovel and fling them into the water between us. The sizzling coals and smoke deter the cranes' approach. In the fading light of the campfire, we see one, then two others, make their move to come ashore. They bump into the net and, with necks retracted and bills turn aside, they patrol left and right as if to go around. The semicircle bow of the net deters this effort, and soon they settle down and grow contented. Eight cranes purr quietly in the dark. We see one, then several tuck their heads into the feathers of their back, then eyelids cover bright corneas, and sleep comes for them and for us.

Once or twice through the night, I stir and check the birds with my flashlight. It seems that one or more is always on the alert watching, wondering, listening for a quiet splash of a paw in the water that separates them from danger.

It's a cloudy, breezy night with a brisk south wind, a good wind for a northbound migration. The winter nights are still long enough that we are anxious to rise when we see the first glow in the east. Tuesday, 12 March dawns. I hop up and wade into the icy water. It is very important to drop the net and get it out of sight before the cranes discover they can go around it.

By 6:00, two cranes bugle and lift off. Then at 6:30, five rise and circle camp. About 7 a.m., seven of our birds walk upstream away from the water and into a weed patch bordering a copse of short, brushy mesquite. It is time to send in the lynx. Roark, still as crane mama, strides quickly south, changes costume, then creeps in from the mesquites. All seven cranes grow alert and, with heads very high, they stride toward the pond. Roark, as Mr. Lynx, rises and hisses, and all seven fan their wings frantically. They circle the area twice, then land in the open flat and for half an hour, they do little but watch very attentively.

At 8 a.m., we hear four rifle shots and the death cry of a rabbit. It sounds as though there is a hunter less than a half mile to the west. Roark grabs the shotgun. I'm armed with the .22. I was under the impression this area was a refuge and closed to hunting, so we stride purposefully on our mission of interception. Soon we are spotted by camo-clad hunters half running, half walking toward a beige Scout. Roark is armed only with a firecracker launcher and I have only a small-bore rifle, so we don't want these guys to get too excited. When we are still 100 yards from their car, I tell Roark to stop, hold the shotgun at the ready, and look mean. I walk in slowly, non-threateningly. As they arrive at their vehicle, so do I. Me: "Hi, how ya doin'? What's up?" The hunters: "We're just camped over there." They try to look calm. They are not doing a very good job of it. I am glad Roark has me backed up with my long tom firecracker gun. They say they are just hunting coyotes and claim it is legal. I don't differ and say goodbye, but before they disappear, I record their license number, FXZ-111, in my notebook.

For the rest of the day, the cranes hang close to camp. Roark and I settle into our crafts. He is scraping on a stone pipe bowl with periodic bouts knapping obsidian. I have brought a walking stick which I harvested two years ago in Maryland. It is one of those how-did-it-get-like-that wonders of the natural world. For three-quarters of its length, it is furrowed, spiral fashion, the result of being "strangled" by a honeysuckle vine. We while away the hours, filing, scraping, sanding, so that by evening, the products of our labors take shape.

Just as the sun touches the ridge of Baboquivari Peak, 60 takes off and all seven follow. They make several long circles with the golden glow on their wings. The crisp hiss of each wing stroke is very audible as they pass overhead. When they land, the sun has disappeared to the west, but it still reddens the Cerro Colorado to the east. It is very quickly cold: we hurry to get a fire going and prepare for the night.

Wednesday, 13 March, dawns early. By 6:00, I don my Russian thigh-high waders and push through the sticky mud into the pond. By 6:10, I have the net down and out of sight so as to not reveal its secret to our cranes. I am up, so I encourage the cranes to be off. At 6:25, I give a loud Gawoww, then run flapping. Seven of the eight run after me, then fly in four grand circles around the pond. Although they fly two to four miles in the circling tour, none of them appear to be planning on going north.

We busy ourselves with breakfast and gear and are rather inattentive to the cranes. When the birds are very near camp, there is no real danger of predator attack, so we can largely ignore them. 86 wanders around the end of our crane excluding fence and finds that the real danger is dead center at mid camp: poking about for bright things to peck at, he plods into the fire circle, then leaps away, very obviously (but insignificantly) burned. This is my favorite bird: I wonder if my reason for favoring him isn't that we share similar Karma . . . I look at him and ponder my broken nose (three times), the bicycle accidents, my motor vehicle smash-ups, the eagle talon wounds, my broken bones, the ricochet bullet I took, my 16-stitches-in-the-head handball court collision . . . maybe 86 is not so accident prone after all.

By 8 a.m., Roark and I have our breakfast out of the way and our gear pretty well defrosted and dry. We are hoping that the cranes get their morning activity period over or fly north so we can migrate ourselves. Just at 8:00, six of our eight birds call, posture, run, then circle camp for a few times. Maybe they will fly north. By 9 a.m., nothing migration-related looks imminent, so we load seven of our eight cranes, then spend twenty minutes trying to convince Miles-Tony that he wants to ride with his buddies. Finally, I outsmart him into going beak-first into a paloverde and we are back on the road again. Our plan is to return the following week and try again.

It's 19 March, time for Crane Migration: Take 3. Roark and I got a rather late start, so it is 6 p.m. before we have all eight cranes loaded and are bouncing our way to Chongo Tank. The sun drops below Mildred Peak before we arrive. Even though it is the end of the day, our cranes are anxious for freedom and the first two that leap from the cranemobile barely touch down before they bound into flight. They make one big circle before the others are out of the truck. Then all eight make two big circles. They are full of excitement and probe the mud for another two hours. For the first half hour as they probe and stroll, I follow along closely behind, inspecting injuries from two weeks ago. My buddy 86 has three wounds and all are pretty well closed, but he is limping a little from last week's campfire burn . . . he will get over it. The neck slasher is mostly healed, as is 10. 116 still has its broken toe strongly deflected right, but the wound is closed and there is no limping.

We have long since dined and readied our sleeping gear before the cranes calm down and march into the roost. The pond is about three inches lower than last week, so by evening light, I wade out and move our net fifteen feet to the north, into deeper water.

It is 20 March and another month will pass before spring comes to the high country, but here in the Altar Valley, spring came last week. I wade out and drop the net half hour before the sun touches the eastern horizon. The birds are awake, flap-happy, and ready to dance. Miles-Tony is the instigator of the first flight, but once the birds are aloft, she drops back.

Roark and I get breakfast, then set up to do our crafts. This week I am making another honeysuckle-choked walking stick. This one is for my wife, Cathy. At 8:15, five of our cranes move to a spot along the shore where they are very vulnerable to predation, so . . . I send in the 'lynx.' Because of the location of the dirt bank, Roark gets within thirty feet before he rises out of the weeds. The cranes freeze with heads up. They are very alarmed, don't take a step for a full two seconds, then all burst into flight simultaneously, circling the pond nine times. Finally they land, but all remain very alert.

Roark and I whittle away the time. Looks like Cathy's spiral-ridged walking stick will be even better than my own. The cranes play, the flies buzz, the hours pass. At 12:15, an adult male merlin flies in and brightens our day. At about 2:30, two subadult golden eagles fly in. One stoops and lands in a mesquite about half mile to the west. After a few minutes, it flies and circles over our pond. It is low enough that a shell cracker might help. Roark launches the projectile. It rises up very near the eagle and explodes. The eagle slowly soars away . . . unconcerned. I am wondering why we brought this gun if it doesn't do any good.

The hours slip away. The cranes seem happy enough to be in the wild, but unconcerned that all of their long-necked conspecifics have left Arizona for cooler climes. At 6 p.m., an adult male harrier drops in and spends a few moments checking out the pond. Near sunset, three cranes launch and circle, then four fly, then these are joined by the other four, so that, just at sunset, all eight are aloft. After a few revolutions, all settle in for the evening.

That evening, I decide that by now our birds are trained to stay in the water overnight, so I leave the net down. Bad idea: the invasion begins. Rather than get out of my bag and do five minutes of wading to get the net in place, I heave shovels full of glowing embers into the shallows. Baka (recently renamed Hari Kari after she sliced her neck) gets frightened and flies off into the dark. She circles three times over camp. By flashlight, I illuminate a landing spot, but she ignores it and disappears into the darkness, bleating. Flashlights scan: there is a large owl on a stump at the far side of the pond. No Baka. We get up, dress, and scour the environs by flashlight, give up, go back to bed. I drop off to sleep wondering if Baka will survive the night.

21 March. No need to rise early to drop the already down net. At first light, the cranes march into camp. They hammer on the welded wire corral, drill my plastic tarp, and in general have a good time at our expense. There are only seven of them: Baka is missing. At 6:15, Baka flies in from the north. All seven rise and join her. A little reunion ensues, but soon all have settled back into the routine.

Breakfast is still underway when all of a sudden, all the birds flare up in excitement and five launch, flying four circles around camp. They pass again and again across the face of Baboquivari Peak, aglow in the early morning sun.

Soon it is time to capture the eight and return them to their pen. We had so much trouble before, capturing Miles-Tony, that I have withheld food since last night. When we plop down the feeder, it is within the welded wire semicircle. Other birds march boldly in to feed, but we capture none until Miles-Tony enters . . . then I pounce. Once she is safely in the belly of the cranemobile, we proceed with the others until all are back in the safety of their pen.

With the failure of our third migration attempt, I am wondering if the cranes have any idea what they are supposed to do. Perhaps Mom and the cranemobile kept them anchored to Chongo Tank when they would otherwise have gone. Whatever the reason for their failure to go north, I have decided that when April comes, I am hauling them to Mormon Lake, then next fall we will see if they know to go south.

Chapter 11

Summer of the Feathered Felons

When Jon Gatlin, a high school freshman, offered to spend his spring vacation helping me release my eight surviving cranes in the mountains of northern Arizona, I accepted. In Arizona, spring comes at various times. Around Tucson (2,400 feet elevation), the cottonwood trees begin to leaf out in February. At Mormon Lake (elevation 7,000 feet), they leaf out in May. To show up at Mormon Lake on 1 April is like giving yourself an April Fool's Day present of a cold or the flu.

It is 7:45 a.m. when I pick up Jon at his home amid the oaks and granite dells that surround our neighborhood. At 10 a.m., we are at the Buenos Aires Refuge and are busy transferring gear to the cranemobile. All of the cranes but Miles-Tony seem happy to join us for another excursion. They have no idea that they are about to go back to winter.

At 11:21, we are loaded and pull out on our way to Flagstaff, 3,500 feet higher and 231 miles further north than the Altar Valley. The travel is uneventful except for two stops to break out the machete and procure a few more coyote chunks. We arrive just early enough to set up camp before dark. It is my decision to place the cranemobile as near as practical to the water. My plan is to camp for two days very near the lake shore just like at Chongo Tank. For these two days we will wear costumes and nurture our birds as they settle in. Thereafter, we will doff our costumes and use shell crackers, mace, and running attacks to teach the birds to avoid humans so they don't go into town. That's Plan A.

Mormon Lake is a 5-mile long elliptical pond surrounded by a doughnut of dense bulrushes and cattails. Although most of the time it is a very shallow pond, Mormon Lake occasionally turns into a huge mud flat. Come spring, broad, flower-dotted meadows extend beyond the lake. These open prairies quickly grade into a ponderosa pine forest with many trees old and grand. The east side of Mormon Lake abuts a volcanic escarpment, a hundred-foot-tall slope of boulders and brush.

One hundred and fifteen years ago, a Mormon elder named Lot Smith (the same man who in 1858 led the militia that burned the Wyoming prairies in front of Johnston's Army as it advanced west to tame the Mormons) established a dairy just west of Mormon Lake. The cows grazed the meadows, rested beneath the spreading pines, and produced the milk and butter that was distributed as far as Saint Joseph (now Joseph City), about seventy miles to the east. While the Mormons occupied the valley, an ornithologist named Edgar Mearns dropped in for a visit. He later reported that sandhill cranes occupied the basin, and he was shown eggs collected in the marshes. Sandhills probably disappeared not long after Mearns' visit and were never again reported to breed in the vicinity, or for that matter, anywhere else in Arizona.

Our cranes seem happy with their new environment: they march off into the marsh, then rise as a group and fly three big circles before landing and marching back to camp. We have only about an hour to work before dark, so we race about finding fuel wood and placing the big red crane feeder at the marsh edge. I walk a half-mile diameter semicircle, strategically placing twelve coyote chunks, hemming us into a "no coyote" zone bordering the marsh.

It is cold even before the sun goes down behind the forested ridge of Mormon Mountain. A frigid breeze blasts under the belly of the cranemobile. John and I pile our food and gear underneath the cranemobile trying to make a solid wall against the wind. By dark, we have a blazing driftwood fire. Seven of the cranes stand statue-like in the near frozen marsh water. Only 116 (Broken Toe) lingers in the circle lighted by our fire. We hunker down, warm inside our sleeping bags, but anxious about the prospects of a cold tomorrow out on this wind dominated flat.

2 April. About 5 a.m., the cranes bugle loudly, then come whooshing over camp. 116 rushes to join them and all eight circle again, but

by 5:30, all eight march into camp and commence stabbing tarps and hammering cans. In addition, there's always the threat of a deposition on one's sleeping bag. For nearly an hour, we fight off the invasion from the warmth of our bags, then at 6:20, the sun crosses the eastern horizon, so we rise, drive the cranes away, then pack gear. The cranes go to the marsh, giving us an hour or so of relief. Then something happens: we do not see any attack, but for the rest of the day, the birds remain skittish. They cower and bunch when even a gull or other small bird passes. I suspect that one of the resident golden eagles has darkened their skies. Later they wander far from camp, but then run and fly to the cranemobile in fright.

All day, we huddle by the car. The wind is incessant. I try to show Jon how to knap flint, but the dust whips around the cranemobile and most of the time we are squinting to keep the dirt out of our eyes. Jon is surviving, but seems somewhat lethargic, even ill. In the evening, we have visitors from the Forest Service. The Forest Service people hang around until dark, so I propose an evening stroll. At 10 p.m., we walk into the dark and see our birds roosting in two groups about forty feet offshore.

Dawn on 3 April begins Phase II, the first day of our "human-avoidance conditioning." At first light, the cranes circle past, then walk into camp, so I rise and shoo them away. Jon must have been sick during the night because there's a frying pan sized pool of vomit just a foot away from his sleeping head. It is frozen solid. Cogs spin: gray matter focuses: I devise a plan. What if when Jon wakes, there is no mess? He will think his night was just a very bad dream. So while Jon sleeps on, I build a sizable fire. Next, I swing the blade on my army shovel to the dig position and lock it into place. My plan is to burn the vomit to ashes so Jon does not have to deal with it and we do not have to move camp. I apply my shovel to the task, but the vomit will not budge. Finally with a little digging, I pry the entire mass up out of the ground. It hangs there, a two-inch thick frozen frisbee. I flop it over so it is easier to look at, then slide it over to the fire. As I pry it over the rocks and into the hungry flames, the heat releases the sour odor and I debate the wisdom of my plan. For the next ten minutes, I stand up wind and watch as the soil, ice, and yesterday's dinner melt and sizzle, then disappear. Now for the rest of my plan. I scoop about here and there, gathering soil from places where its absence will not be noticed.

Next, I pack it firmly into the frisbee crater. Then I make a whisk broom from nearby bulrushes and obliterate all sign that the frisbee had ever existed. Jon sleeps on, the fire quits sizzling, the plan is in place.

I stumble around camp packing gear and wishing for spring. There are two inches of ice in the dishwater and lots of frost on my sleeping gear. I notice that Miles-Tony has an ice ball on her radio antenna, revealing the water depth at her nighttime roost. None of the cranes have frozen discs on their legs although these often form when cranes roost in water on very cold nights. I remember reading that ankle-deep ice water was sometimes used in Gulag prison camps as a torture technique . . . perhaps one would have to use hot water for cranes.

By 9 a.m., I am all packed and anxious to move camp. Now that we are supposed to be weaning our cranes away from human contact, the plan is to move our camp into the protection of the forest. Jon rouses, peers down at the ground where his vomit once reposed, looks away, looks back in disbelief, says nothing, processes the information, and goes down to try for more sleep. When he rouses again, I help him and his bag into the shelter of the pines. To keep the cranes from homing in on our new camp, we left the tent out on the flat with a crane costume attached, flapping in the wind. To keep the wind from migrating our tent into the lake, I packed it full of firewood.

Our cranes look okay out on the marsh. Apparently Jon is going to sleep all day and he needs some pain relief, so I leave him in his sleeping bag, jump into the cranemobile, and head for Flagstaff. I buy mace and aspirin, bathe, and check for messages. Then I pick up some "crane alert" fliers from the Forest Service and go to the hotel in the little burg called Mormon Lake Village and distribute the fliers so the locals will understand our project.

At 5:30 p.m., I drive through camp and then leave the cranemobile out in the marsh so the cranes can use it as a base. At 6 p.m., Jon and I do our first bout of attacking the cranes. First we get rid of our costumes, then we let them walk very close, then I spray mace on three of them. They blink a little, then ignore it. Jon and I withdraw, load the shotgun, and charge. I fire three shell crackers at the confused birds. They flee, but only half heartedly. Jon's feeling better, so I send him in screaming and running. The cranes obligingly fly fifty yards or so, but are very unconvinced. We retreat and leave them puzzling over our changed demeanor.

After Jon and I set up camp, we have some time to talk. Jon asks me what I know about the disappearing vomit. I 'fess up: he thinks it is funny, but is not well enough to laugh.

Tonight is the first night we have slept far from the cranes, so at 9:30, we walk out to see if they are in the water. The moon is nearly full. All eight stand well out from the shore, but when 116 detects us, she begins to rapidly approach. I can imagine how much fun it is to stand in freezing water with a broken toe. Apparently four others share her feelings because now we have five cranes closing in on us. What to do? We back off, wait until all five are on terra firma, then I charge at them swinging my jacket. Three fly: two splash off into the darkness. I whack myself between the eyes with the big double zipper on my jacket . . . a warm dark liquid runs down my face. We wait a few minutes in the dark wondering where the three will end up. I mop at my forehead. They call quietly: we hear their wing strokes as they pass over twice. The moon glistens softly on their wings. Finally, they settle into the lake next to their flock mates. We creep away, hoping to avoid attracting them shoreward again. At length, a black clot congeals on my forehead.

Back beneath the canopy of the forest, Jon and I settle into our snug sleeping bags with the glow of the campfire warming our faces. Sleep comes easily. Three times during the night, I am awakened to the rusty hinge bugles of small bands of elk crossing the meadow to our east. They are on their way to drink at the lake. In the night, the bands have the appearance of huge black caterpillars rushing north. In the early morning light, we see them returning south to the forest. Mostly they are cows and calves, but some are bulls with mid-sized antlers.

4 April dawns gray and threatening. This will be Day 2 of our human-avoidance training. By 6:00 we see the cranes far away making their morning flight. At 6:40, I stalk in with my shotgun but see seven of the eight sheltering near the cranemobile, a practice I choose to encourage, so I slip away without disturbing them.

When I approach at 8:20, I see all of them at the marsh edge, so I creep in to make my attack. When about 50 m away, I lob a shell cracker near them. At the pop, all heads go up but none fly, so I quickly place another round in the chamber and fire. Again they show alarm and this time they see me running at them, screaming and waving, so all eight run into flight and make a long, slow circle. Five continue to fly, but the others land near me. The five aloft begin to circle down and approach me, so I lob another shell cracker. I time it so that it passes through the flock and explodes behind them, pushing them on past me. They land in the water and eye me from a distance, unable to comprehend why it is that Mom looks so strange and is behaving so aggressively. I tally up one very successful bout of human-avoidance-conditioning and saunter back to camp.

Jon is better, and although the day is rather miserable, he contents himself reading around a constantly fed fire. I settle down and busy myself working on a manuscript. The hours drag by. I am only planning on two or three attack sessions per day, so we just wait until afternoon.

At 12:30, the cranes come to see us. Seven of our eight birds circle up to about 700 feet and drift south of the lake until they are over the meadow just east of our forest camp. They seem to be carried along by the winds fronting a snow squall. This is our "training opportunity," so Jon and I hurry out into the meadow with my Long Tom. We are going to see if we can tempt them down by our presence and we are going to teach them a lesson if they succumb. Good news! They remain aloft, then drift north to the shore and parachute down near the cranemobile.

As the afternoon wears on, Jon is demonstrating his teenage energy, so I send him for a hike through the woods to Mormon Lake Village. About 4:30, he returns and he is not alone. He has picked up an escort of two black Labrador retrievers. As camp is being invaded by two overly friendly canines, my first response is anger. But in an instant, I see an opportunity in the making. The dogs have already followed Jon for about a mile: maybe they will go with us for another half.

I grab the shotgun and all four of us head for the lake. We quickly notice that the dogs prefer to run ahead of us at about 100 yards. They adjust their course to stay more-or-less directly ahead of us and that far away. We proceed by "steering" the dogs toward the lake but south and east of a tall bulrush bed so the cranes cannot see them. Then, when the dogs are about thirty yards from the cranes, we swing them around and move directly toward the birds. The dogs rush about, plunging through the bulrushes immediately between us and the cranes. All eight birds burst into flight and circle up to about a thousand feet. They break into two groups but continue to circle for about twenty minutes.

Not wanting to cause a long distance movement of our birds, we "lead" our dogs south and west away from the lake. As we rush along, we converge with Mr. Ed VerBeck and his yellow Lab. Mr. VerBeck is a longtime resident of Mormon Lake Village, cherishes the area's pristine state, and wants to know who is responsible for putting the cranemobile on the lake bed. I confess, but then listen to a barely contained tirade about the virtues of leaving nature free of truck tracks. He announces his intention of reporting me to the Forest Service and marches promptly away without allowing me to respond. I march along behind him urging/demanding that he hear my explanation. He listens to my story about the return of the sandhill crane, changes from hostile to supportive, and leaves as a friend. It takes me a few moments to clear the adrenalin out of my blood stream. For a few anxious moments, I thought there was going to be a fist fight. Then I remembered . . . I have a 12-gauge shotgun in my arms. The two black Labs follow Ed and his yellow dog across the meadow and back into the forest.

In the late evening, we wander out to see if our cranes are okay. By flashlight, we see seven (or could it be all eight) in water, but not far from shore.

When we awake on 5 April, we discover an inch of snow on the tarps covering our sleeping bags. There are seventeen or so elk crossing the meadow to our east. The sky is gray and blustery. Snow blankets the landscape, and the prospects of a warm, sunny day are gone. Maybe we migrated too soon to the high country. By 6:15, I am up and checking on the cranes. Seven huddle around the cranemobile. Fortunately, last night we covered our supply of firewood with a tarp, so in short order we have a crackling blaze underway. By 7:00, the clouds close in: we are enveloped in a whiteout. The snow flurries quickly pass but leave us feeling apprehensive of the day ahead. This will be our last day with our cranes, so we hope they are wed to the site and can survive the coyotes and nighttime elk attacks.

Our human-avoidance training has gone pretty well, so I am hopeful that the birds will not invade the village after we leave. At 10 a.m., I take the shotgun and a bag of crane food and set out to train the birds.

I am also going to move the cranemobile to higher ground, but as we have learned to expect, it will not start. The battery drain problem has reappeared, so I am forced to leave it only 100 feet from the water. This translates into two inches above lake level. I fill the feeder half full, then begin my stalk at the cranes. I run in screaming and shooting, but they just fly off 100 yards and show only mild alarm. Ms. Broken Toe, 116, actually responds to my charge by walking toward me. I rush at her, swinging the empty food sack over my head, so she runs and glides ahead of me only half convinced that I am in any way dangerous. If she will not run from me, I must run from her, so I turn and jog away, uncertain that our cranes are going to stay out of trouble until my return.

Early that afternoon, Cathy arrives in another car to transport Jon and me the 255 miles home. Eight cranes probe the icy marshes. They probe because they are genetically programmed to do so, even though food is still a month away. As we drive away, Mormon Lake is still locked in winter's grip. Within an hour, we enter a desert already firmly locked in summer.

Our cranes made Mormon Lake their home: you could almost always count on seeing some or all of them at the south end of the lake. Early in the evening on 10 April, Tracy Herbert and I rolled through the tongue of woods that points north toward Mormon Lake. We moved quickly to set up camp, then went out to count our birds . . . five (but only five) were roosting in water at the south end of the lake. We scanned with our radio receiver, but only five signals could be detected. While Tracy filled the feeder, I busied myself installing a fully-charged battery in the cranemobile. It cranked over in its faltering, heart-stopping sort of way, then sprang to life. We moved it to safety on higher ground.

As darkness fell, we heaped our campfire higher and prepared for a cool, clear night. Our beef stew sat at the edge of the bright ring, temperature slowly rising. Every ten minutes, we donned a leather glove, plucked the cans from the ashes, gave them a good sloshing, then redeposited them with the other side facing the fire. After two or three bouts of sloshing and heating, the lid begins to bulge and you know it is time to either pluck your dinner from the flames or take cover. Wait too long, and the whole campsite is bombarded with carrots and potatoes. When safely removed from the flames, shake the can lightly, then let it stand until the lid begins to return to its pre-bulging form. Then it's time to de-cap-itate and devour. Some seasoned campers will probably think this method (which we lovingly entitle the Pat Ryan pressure cooker for its inventor, the bear biologist from the Navajo Indian Reservation) a bit strange, but once you've tried it, you're hooked. No dirty pans and after extracting the contents, you just toss the can in the fire to cremate the remnants. In the morning, you fish the can out of the ashes, stomp it flat (rocks work well if you are barefoot and fear lid lacerations), and bingo, you tote out odor-free trash.

A half mile away, five cranes stand on one leg in 40°F water. Something moves in the darkness and they trumpet their alarm. I rouse, blink dully at the embers of the fire, focus on the crane calls, decide that they did not fly, glance at the eastern sky, note the position and phase of the moon, decide it is about 3 a.m., and I collapse into deep sleep. Five seconds have elapsed.

When morning really comes, we go out to check on our cranes. Still only five are present. They are 86, Baka, and three friends. We scan with our receiver, but still only find five. It looks like Miles-Tony, Broken Toe, and one other crane have vanished. We decide to try for yet another method of human avoidance conditioning. This time we hunker down, approach in a sideways-don't-look-at-'em fashion, and circle closer and closer until we are within five yards. The birds are rather skittish, so I realize it is now or never. I wait until 229, the nearest crane, looks away, then with a half-second advantage, rush out with an electric cattle prod in my left hand, jab her in the flank, push the electrocute button, then watch her and the group flap away. There was a sickening squish when I jabbed 229 in the side, but no indication that she actually got a shock. Worse yet, the thing could cause serious trauma after the electrodes probe through the feathers. Something tells me that I spent $60 on a bad idea. I'm gonna get my money back.

Later that morning, I try again to teach the cranes to not trust humans. I sit on the big boulder by the feeder and lure all five cranes close to me by tossing pellets. This time, in a more controlled fashion, I gently lay the prod for about two seconds against 10's leg. Nothing. Next, I gently jab another bird. Still nothing happens. I am taking this thing back to the vendor.

Having failed at the stealth and shock method, Tracy and I revert to the shotgun. At 9:02, we rush in on the cranes. As Tracy sprints after them, I cock the single gun and launch a cracker that explodes thirty yards from the cranes. They rise up to 1,000 feet, then in lazy circles they slowly drift to the west. After about twelve minutes, they whoosh down and land only forty yards from the feeder. An hour later, the cranes, alarmed by something on the ground, take off and soar. They are still aloft when we exit to search for the missing three.

At midday, we pick up a weak signal from Broken Toe, far to the east. We violate the first rule of radio telemetry and begin hiking toward the source (you are supposed to triangulate a location by getting two converging bearings before you close in). There are no roads to use, so we just start hiking east. The bird is not in the first valley, so we hike to the next forested ridge, listen again, and realize she must be very far away.

By the time we arrive back at my Scout, a huge dark gray cloud mass obscures the San Francisco Peaks and is quickly bearing down on us. It is dense like a summer thunderhead, but the color and extent of the cloud mass and the bitter wind that proceeds it tells us it is a winter blizzard. At 12:30, we position ourselves on the bluff overlooking the lake and quickly check on our group of five. All are on dry ground, standing by the cranemobile.

Next we make a desperate attempt to find our missing three. We bounce east on the dirt road to Kinnikinick Lake. A herd of about thirty elk passes through the forest. Snow begins: no signals: wisdom tells us to get off the mountain. We turn the Scout toward warmer skies, and within half an hour we are ahead of the storm. That evening, we camp in the fragrant desert: Tracy seems glad to heat his stew to bulging on a campfire of saguaro cactus ribs.

On 13 April, safely home in Oracle, I am wondering about my missing cranes and catching up on paperwork when a call comes through that one of our three missing cranes has shown up on the San Carlos Apache Reservation at a wide place in the road called Geronimo. This is 150 miles southeast of Mormon Lake. My best guess is that this crane saw that big blizzard the same way we did and headed for warmer country.

The next day, I am in Safford, Arizona retrieving 320 from wildlife rehabilitators, Tony and Jerry Williams. Our crane is very thin, only 2,700 grams (6 pounds). The cranemobile is parked at Mormon Lake, so I have to use Plan B to transport this bird. Plan B requires pulling a pant leg over the crane, then taping or pinning the crotch end closed so the crane does not escape. It is very dark when 320 and I arrive at Mormon Lake. Her transmitter needs to be changed, so she must spend the night confined in her pant leg on the pine needle carpet just a few feet from my sleeping bag.

When morning comes, 320 seems happy enough, pecking at the crane pellet pile. Very quickly, I put on her new radio and release her on the meadow by camp. She seems wobbly at first, but rouses and shakes her feathers three times, then walks slowly away. After ten minutes, I decide to rush her to see if she can fly. She only runs, so I circle in and capture her, then carry her the half mile to the lake shore. She seems happy to be at the feeder but unfortunately now there is only one bird to join her. It is 10, the big male. The battery in my receiver is too low for me to see if the other cranes are around, so I leave '10' and 320 and rush to Flagstaff to charge my receiver.

It is late that night before I return with my receiver all charged up. Up before the sun, I scan the shoreline for cranes. I see four! I see five! I walk out and see a sixth also, but who are they? It is 86, Baka, Broken Toe, 10, 211, and 320, our bird retrieved from Geronimo. So where are Miles-Tony and 229? For the rest of the morning, Chuck LaRue and I are either searching for our lost two or attacking the six with cracker shells. Unbeknownst to us, Miles-Tony and 229 have already been found, but I have to wait a day and drive 255 miles home to learn that 229 is then in Flagstaff, only twenty miles from Mormon Lake, and Miles-Tony is gaining new friends at Bonita Creek, about forty miles south of Mormon Lake. My friend from twenty years ago, John Goodwin, an Arizona Game and Fish Department biologist captures 229 at the golf course and on 18 April returns her to Mormon Lake.

While we were searching for Miles-Tony, she was enjoying a tuna fish lunch in the home of a Mrs. Sumter. Josh Taiz, a Forest Service employee, called me the next day. Josh seemed brave, near, and willing, so I saved myself the 500-mile round trip: I authorized him to ferry the crane home to Mormon Lake. Josh later informed me that Miles rode quietly in the pant leg of a nomex firefighter's suit, with a seat belt snugly attached.

As the pieces of the puzzle trickled in through the months, I realized that the reason we know so well where and when our cranes traveled was not because of their radios, but because of their tameness.

Sadly, shortly after 229's trip to Flagstaff, she was found dead near the road edge west of Mormon Lake. This was our first mortality since the migration the previous fall. Seven birds survived her at Mormon Lake and as we soon learned, Dennis, the Disturbed, lost during the migration, is still alive at the Hassayampa River Reserve near the Vulture Mountains where she went missing in October.

The next week as I crossed over Mingus Mountain in the course of my ramblings to make crane-related arrangements, I got one of the most convincing flat tires I have ever seen. I heard the sizzling noise and got my plugging kit open and ready, then I began pulling on the head of what turned out to be a quarter-inch diameter nail. All six inches of it emerged from my tire. The next day I pulled a fencing staple out of another tire, and that same day, two feed sacks fell against my spare tire and broke the valve stem. In two days, I got more flats than most people get in a year.

Around noon on 24 April, I arrived at the south end of Mormon Lake. All seven cranes were hanging around the cranemobile, so I decided on a little human-avoidance trickery. With loaded shotgun, and while still far away, I circled slowly to the non-crane side of the cranemobile. When completely out of view to the cranes, I charged. As I sprinted around the hood, the cranes scattered like popcorn on a hot stove. Boom . . . boom: I sent them pumping away. In a way it is really sad to be attacking your crane buddies, especially my pal '86', but, then again, when the hunter instinct kicks in, you enjoy charging in and watching them flee. I also knew that if I did not somehow make them wild, they would sooner or later all get into trouble. After terrifying my cranes, I checked the feeder. Spring was formally here and the cranes still were eating lots of our pelletized diet, but not as much as the feeder indicated. From tracks and scattered food, it looked a lot like the raccoons had found a free lunch. I moved the red cylinder fifty meters away and tucked it into a bulrush patch.

Two more times that day, I attacked my birds, then sat in my Scout doing paperwork and watching their movements. At 5 p.m., Broken Toe lies down. When the group forages away, she remains lying and big 10 returns and remains with her. Is she sick? Are they a pair? 86 seems to be the leader of the main group. Miles-Tony remains on the periphery of the main group. About 6 p.m., Broken Toe is up and does a right-left stomp and begins to dance. Big 10 also stomps, then bobs around in pre-dance.

Poor Miles-Tony: she spends much time alone and when she flies to rejoin the group at 7:01 p.m., three cranes rush her and she flutters away. My cranes remind me of people. Following a cloudy sunset, the six (all except Broken Toe) march off to the marsh. Finally, Broken Toe follows. Fifteen minutes later, all seven rise up, circle three times, then land in the water. It is time for them to roost and me also. I exit for camp.

This night, and most other nights that I have camped by Mormon Lake, when it gets completely dark, a vehicle can be detected near the paved road south of the lake. Sometimes I can hear the engine, but mostly I just see a powerful spotlight scanning left and right across the meadow and up into the forest. I have never heard a shot fired and I do not know what they are seeking, but this kind of behavior very often bespeaks poaching. It is also concentrated on that part of the forest from which the elk appear but . . . who knows?

At 5:30 a.m., 25 April, I am awakened to see eleven elk crossing the meadow. Ten adults easily leap over the barbed wire fence, but one yearling paces for five minutes, then goes between the wires. An hour later, fifteen mule deer, a group of twenty-five elk, and the group of eleven elk all forage in the south end of the meadow.

The next day, I try three more attacks on my cranes. It seems that they are always suckers for the whiz-around-the-cranemobile trick. Today I tried an interesting variation. First I hid in the cranemobile. Then when the cranes approached, I slipped out the far door, and zoomed around to chase them.

I have noticed that the cranes are often very nervous and watch the sky as if expecting attack. Sometimes when they are upset, they rush to the cranemobile, not a bad strategy to evade an attacking eagle or coyote. We occasionally see a pair of eagles hunting the bluff that runs seven miles along the east side of the lake. We only once observed them attempt to capture a crane, but from the cranes' behavior, I would guess they have tried.

Another thing I noticed today; Miles-Tony, our most subordinate crane, has a cut and swelling in her right lore, the soft area between the base of the bill and the eye. She also retains more juvenile plumage than any of the other cranes. For example, she has an inch-wide belt of gray feathers on her crown. All of the other cranes have long since lost these feathers and have only red papillaceous skin on their now very adult-like crowns. I watch Miles-Tony and wonder if beat-up, submissive, adolescent humans are also slower to develop.

At sunset, I count my seven cranes in the roost area, fill the crane feeder, and sprint for home. It is half an hour after midnight before I stumble into bed.

One week later, I drive back north. Chuck LaRue is to meet me at Mormon Lake. When I arrive, Chuck is missing, so I park conspicuously, then hike the old roadbed on the east side of the lake. A yearling peregrine falcon circles over very close. I think about the old records of peregrine falcons being seen in summer at Mormon Lake and wonder where they nested. Was it on the low bluffs above the lake or on some other crag? Or is it possible that they used an old hawk nest in a tree, like peregrines sometimes do in Germany, southwestern Canada, Australia, and a few other places. Perhaps peregrines never bred at Mormon Lake, but if they did, I'll bet they will soon return. There is a great increase in peregrine populations underway in the western U.S. and it is nowhere more apparent than in Arizona. And in Arizona it is happening without the release of captive-reared chicks to supplement recovery of the wild populations. I consider the hundred plus years that have passed since cranes bred here. Oh, how I want some of our birds to be the vanguard. Wouldn't it be great if '86' was the founder of a line?

But for now, we need to keep these juveniles home and out of trouble. Speaking of trouble, Pandora's box is about to be opened. Remember Dennis, the ill-mannered nemesis of last fall's migration? A big reason we have tolerated Miles-Tony so long is that we can easily remember that Dennis was far worse. Well, Dennis spent the winter with The Nature Conservancy, but has grown too difficult for them. I agree to have her join our birds at Mormon Lake. Another of my bad ideas.

That evening, Chuck and I have enough problems even without Dennis. After sunset but before dark, we see six cranes at the cranemobile. Could they really be roosting out of the water? Three times we rush the birds hoping they will move to water. On the last rush, they disappear in the dark going north over water. So . . . ?

Next morning, we begin our watch at 4:50 a.m. No cranes are visible by the cranemobile or along the near shore. At 5:42, we are relieved to see our six cranes fly in from the northwest. At 9:30, Val Little and two other women arrive from Wickenburg with Dennis on board. They stop at the Forest Service boundary and we let Dennis hop out of their camper. She rouses, then walks expectantly toward our six. The six march toward her. They see it is Dennis and all six rush at her. She flies off south to safety. Val and friends decide they would like to see what happens next, so the three of them climb into the cranemobile, watch for three-quarters of an hour, then walk to their car and leave.

Shortly after their exit, Dennis walks to the Mormon Lake Guard Station and stands twenty yards from a bunch of Indian kids (working this summer as fire fighters) playing basketball. I creep in, circle nonchalantly until five meters from Dennis, then pounce and wrestle the bird under my control. In retrospect, I should have, at that moment, sent Dennis to the happy hunting ground. For the next fifteen minutes, Dennis mumbles her contempt as I carry her to the crane feeder in the marsh. She seems exhausted, so I just leave her lying near the feeder.

Chuck and I spend an hour circling Mormon Lake listening for radio signals from '229' and Miles-Tony. Nothing. When we return to the cranemobile, we see Dennis still lying down. I rush at her to check for reactions. She rises and walks into the reeds, so I decide she is probably okay.

For the next hour, Chuck and I slog around in the sticky mud installing what we term the "scare-eagle." The scare-eagle is merely a wooden cross pushed into the muddy lake bed and draped with a crane costume. It also has guy wires to keep it vertical in the northern Arizona wind. (Like its namesake, the scare-eagle flutters in the wind and serves to keep eagles from attacking our cranes.) The mud sucks so tenaciously at my boots that I walk out of them and complete the operation barefoot. My plan is to wean the cranes off the cranemobile and onto the scare-eagle to break the bad habit they are developing of roosting out of the water by the cranemobile.

After the scare-eagle is in place, I decide to check on Dennis again. We think it is important that she learn before dark, that there is water nearby, so we try to herd her to water. She flies into the open meadow; we circle and herd; she flies further into the open meadow; we try again; she moves east into the forest; we try again; she climbs through the fence, then runs out onto the highway. I try to outsmart her, but she flies, slope-soars 500-700 feet over the bluff, apparently planning to go back to the Indian basketball game, but lands by our camp and marches into the forest with Chuck in pursuit. Next, Dennis flies out of the forest and west toward the motel near Mormon Lake Village. Chuck and I go our separate ways that afternoon with Dennis still playing juvenile delinquent and nowhere near the marsh.

Two weeks later (19 May), I am on my way back north full of apprehension about my crane flock now that Dennis is part of the equation. As I am filling my gas tank near Picacho Peak, I hear the sizzle of a leaky tire. Without stopping the flow of gas, I extract the nail and insert a plug without causing my fellow customers to wait even one extra second. This tire-plugging kit was one of my wisest investments.

It is 10:14 p.m., when I arrive at my camp site at the edge of the forest at the south end of Mormon Lake. By flashlight, I hike out and check the feeder, note two geese where my cranes should be, then go to camp and sleep. At about 5:30 a.m. on 20 May, I awaken to see five cranes standing in my camp. What is happening? These birds are getting tamer, rather than wilder. I hassle the birds out of camp, then coerce the cranemobile into running and drive it into Flagstaff for repairs.

Over the next few days, reports trickle in. It is not only the cranemobile that needs repairs. On 21 May, I learn that Baka/Hari Kari was found the previous day with a broken leg at Ashurst Lake, about three miles northeast of Mormon Lake. The bird was taken to rehabilitator Christy Van Cleave who adopts Baka, gives her the finest vet care, and moves the bird into her bedroom. Hoping the other missing cranes were with Baka, I do a radio search at Ashurst Lake and neighboring lakes. Nothing.

That evening just before sunset, I stand on the rim of the bluff and sweep the south end of Mormon Lake with binoculars. There are three cranes by the scare-eagle. After a few moments, they delicately lift off the water, fly a half circle and land by two other cranes. All five stand in eight inches of water about 100 yards from shore. So we have at least five cranes, and they are in the water of the correct lake. I make a rash decision: I'm going home. When still a half hour north of Phoenix, I can hardly keep my head up. I realize that, if I continue south, I will die on the highway tonight. I take the first exit, spot a dirt turnoff, cut my lights, creep into the dark desert, gobble a can of luke-warm peaches, and plop down on my sleeping bag. In the darkness, I can see Table Mountain about two miles southeast of me.

About all I can do now is wait. We enter the summer with big plans for our cranes establishing themselves at Mormon Lake. I plan to visit the cranes weekly, or less often if my friends continue to give me reports, but still I watch anxiously as the satellite data comes in. In a few days, I get a weird satellite fix claiming that my little flock has flown a hundred miles east and is north of Snowflake, Arizona. Not likely. But then a few days later, I get a report that Dennis has been hanging around a Navajo hogan near Elephant Butte and near the location of the satellite fix. By the time of the telephone call, Dennis has been moved to the Window Rock Zoo, so I make plans for her retrieval to Mormon Lake . . . not a good idea.

On 31 May, a phone call comes in from Phil Smith, my liaison with the Arizona Game and Fish Department. It seems that four of my cranes are at the Antelope Hills Golf Course, a few miles north of Prescott, Arizona and fifty-eight miles west of Mormon Lake. As of 5 p.m., they were at the residence of Martha Duck. I thank Phil, apolo-gize, and call Ms. Duck. It was then I discovered that Martha loves the big birds and hopes they will stay. I mutter something about coming to see them, then hang up and make plans.

Very early in the morning of 3 June, there are about twenty elk crossing the meadow at Mormon Lake. My son, Merlin and I walk out onto the flat. Merlin wears a crane costume (for warmth). My buddy 86 flies to within 100 yards of us. I decide to see why he is alone and so tame. With food in hand, I creep in and lure him to me. Eventually, I get so close that he can tap crane pellets from my hand. With the other hand, I check his breast. He is dangerously thin. Could he be suffering from "hardware disease" from ingesting the pop rivet in March? The crane feeder is empty. I fill it and move it near the scare eagle. Merlin and I say goodbye to 86 and drive on to Flagstaff where we say good-bye to each other. He turns east on his own odyssey. I rush west, hop-ing that it is not difficult to find the Duck residence.

Martha Duck is not home, but my four cranes are loafing in the shade on the golf course behind her house. I position my Scout, lay out the transport materials (four pant legs and some safety pins) and begin herding cranes. An elderly neighbor offers to help, but he is not fast enough to catch the birds so I use him to block the escape route. Three young bucks from the grounds maintenance crew are attracted by all the calling and running, so I deputize them and very soon all four cranes are trussed up and lying in the furrows and valleys of the equipment pile in my Scout. It is noon and getting warm as I thank all and turn my Scout back on the road. For the next two hours, I keep my Mexican air conditioner (spray bottle) busy squirting legs and bills as I rush on to Mormon Lake.

At the lake, I deputize a botanist and a firefighter and soon we have the four cranes processed and released at the edge of the forest. I decide to let three of the birds stand in the shade and recover from their trip, because 217 has of late appeared partial to 86. I herd her the half mile out to see him. Both seem excited, pleased to see each other, then 86 tucks his head again and dozes on one leg while standing in the water. There's something very wrong with him, but I do not know what.

Considering the bizarre peregrinations of my cranes, you can understand my trepidation when I arrived at Mormon Lake one summer morning with my supervisor, Dr. George Gee, visiting from Maryland. Unbelievable! Six cranes stood there next to the scare-eagle. Even Dennis is there, snugly integrated into the flock.

July passed quietly: my gruiphonaphobia (i.e., fear that the ring of the telephone will require a rush trip to the nether corners of the state to retrieve cranes) began to subside. It was 12 August that I next saw my charges. All six (Miles-Tony now was believed to be residing in crane heaven and Baka was still in the rehabilitation center recovering from her broken leg) were dutifully attending the south end of Mormon Lake. For once, I was glad they were still tame. The satellite transmitter on 86 had recently died, so I lured him in with sliced apple and pounced. He seems in much better condition now and weighs almost twelve pounds. All the birds seem contented and well fed, so I decide to not fill their feeder, an unfortunate decision.

What I forgot to mention earlier was that Dennis broke her bill on somebody's front porch last October and now her bill tips do not meet. With her scissor-faced overbite, she cannot pick up small objects with any accuracy, so she has been very dependent on the grab-and-gulp feeding strategy, only possible with a pile of food. With the feeder

151

gone, Dennis finds gustatorial solace in the goose yard of a human resident at the Village of Mormon Lake. Worse yet, the other five cranes have learned to tolerate Dennis, so now they follow her to easy pickings in town.

While a crane invasion doesn't sound all that threatening, let me tell you what really happens when even a single crane shows up on your doorstep. Our crane migrations are strictly voluntary, so when a bird wants to drop out there is sometimes not much you can do about it. After a radio search, you just wait until the phone rings and a faraway and plaintive voice unfolds another sad tale. So when 321, a bird very like Dennis, abandoned our team, I thought I knew what to expect.

Several days after 321 was lost, I got a phone call from John Nelssen (my phone number is clearly printed on each legband transmitter). This is how the story went. It seems that 321 just plopped down and walked up to the Nelssen ranch house, twenty-five miles from Wickieup and not too much further from Nothing, Arizona (population 5). Nobody and no animal knew how to react, so 321 just sorta took over. John Nelssen said the crane liked chicken food (and towered over the chickens) so the chickens now spend all their time in their house. Maggie Nelssen added, "We haven't had an egg for ten days . . . but that's okay." The Nelssens train show dogs, so their pointer knew just what to do when 321 arrived. He approached and went on point: 321 just flared her wings, hissed, and zapped the dog on the head with her bill. Same thing (except for pointing) happened to the cat. Now both dog and cat creep along, constantly looking over their shoulder for 321. The Nelssens interjected, "But that's okay." Even the big animals have changed habits: the cows no longer come around the house and John says, "The horses have moved to the far corner of their twenty-acre pasture." Then John got punctured in the arm when the tried to move the bird. The house also took minor damage. First 321 was thumping on the glass, then she poked holes in the screen on the bathroom window so she could thump the shampoo bottles. John quickly added, "But that's okay. We needed to replace the screen anyhow."

As the story progressed, I occasionally mumbled apologies and offered to provide a sack of chicken food, but not knowing the cost difference between a champion show dog and a punctured, neurotic mutt, I grew more and more anxious. Finally, a really odd thing happened:

John asked if we were going to do a repeat experiment next year. I quickly and defensively assured him that we were never again going to burden him with another crane, but then he expressed disappointment saying that by next year he will have a two-acre pond for a whole flock of cranes. My final words reflected my relief that John and Maggie had mentioned no plans for hiring a lawyer.

It is 30 August and it's my job to tackle the crane invasion problem head on. I arrive at the recreational vehicle park at the Village of Mormon Lake and see Dennis by a motor home, scarfing down bread. To the north, I see my five other cranes in the meadow. I circle in and grab Dennis by the bustle. Compulsively my fingers reach for the neck vertebrae. My love for cranes restrains me, and somehow I know the animal rights cops would put me away for a very long time, especially if I made my move here in retirement city.

Gently I cradle the "precious" crane in my lap and I drive one-handed to the southeast end of Mormon Lake. I carry Dennis to the refilled feeder. I plan to release her here so she can eat here, know to eat here, stay here, and not lead my other cranes into town. But no, Dennis absolutely ignores the feeder and flies a half mile back toward town. Unarticulated, but not unthought, the words rise up . . . "should've shot her."

When I awaken the next morning, I watch elk crossing the meadow, returning from a much dwindled Mormon Lake. More than a hundred pass before I leave. By 6:30, I am in the RV park stalking my "wild" cranes. Very quickly, I managed to capture 86, then the second male. I transport both to the feeder, then go back to town. By now, the cranes are wise to me. Other people can walk right up to them, but I can't get within twenty feet. I decide on Plan B: spray 'em in the eyes with lemon juice. I am experimenting with various concentrations of juice, with and without methyl anthranilate (grape soda favor . . . nice when mixed one to a million but when taken straight it is a powerful oral deterrent). I blast my birds in the face with my super soaker, then adjust the mixture and blast again. Nothing seems to make the birds do more than rub their eyes on their back a few seconds, so I decide to test it on myself. I turn the gun into my face and let fly. For the next ten minutes, I am flushing my eyes and cursing my idiocy: finally, the burning goes away.

So here I am mixing my next potion on the hood of my car when a very husky cowboy and a fifteen-pounds-heavier-than-her-Levi's-can-handle cowgirl ride up on their horses. I am fifty feet from the cranes and so involved with my squirt gun that they don't connect me with the big birds. The cowboy takes up a position forty feet from the cranes. His lasso dangles from his right hand. He says to his woman, "Cut one out." She rides toward the cranes, huddled in a tight bunch near the fence. Now I'm twenty years older and twenty pounds lighter than the guy with the rope, but I'm red-eyed and armed with righteous indignation and a grape-lemon squirt gun, so without a second thought, I spit out the words, "Are you fixin' to rope a crane?" He looks at me, considers the prospects of explaining to his friends that he is doing jail time for crane molestation, and judiciously says, "No." My courage swells and I spit out a very convincing, "That's good," and stand there, feet wide apart, ready for action, watching the equestrian pair mutter softly to each other as they ride away.

This weekend is the Mormon Lake rodeo and I have seen enough to know that I don't want my birds in the middle of it. I also don't want to hang around civilization brandishing a five-pound squirt gun . . . so I deputize Grant. Grant is a nine-year-old, freckle-energized Phoenician (i.e., a resident of Phoenix, Arizona) up at the village for the rodeo. I give Grant, his brother, and his dad a lecture on the dangers of squirt guns (especially the lemon juice variety) and on the fine art of crane stalking. Grant grabs the gun and zooms in with great speed and accuracy, chasing the cranes out into the meadow. Satisfied, I cast the fate of my six birds to a whirlwind named Grant and head out of town.

In August, Baka finally gave up the struggle. For the last few weeks, she had been living in Christy Van Cleave's bedroom. Following the loss, Christy cried for two days. Cranes almost never survive a broken leg, even with the best veterinary care.

It's 11 September when I check again for my cranes. We drive into Mormon Lake Village and search. Only Dennis is visible. A cowboy named Earl Morgan has been feeding Dennis, and although the crane trusts Earl, Dennis knows we mean trouble so she stays well away from us. After a half hour of trying to corner Dennis between house trainers and motor homes, we finally discuss the problem with Earl. He agrees to help. Earl stands nonchalantly by the corral fence as we herd

Dennis his way. At the last second, Earl's big hands lurch out and Dennis is once again in our power. We drive her out to the feeder near the south end of the lake and try to show her the food. She refuses to eat and just flies away . . . back toward the village. At times like this, it is a good thing my rifle is back at the car.

All of the time, effort, and embarrassment of the summer was endured so we could provide an opportunity for our cranes to fly south in the fall. During migration time the previous spring at Chongo Tank, the cranemobile and crane mamas always remained on the ground, luring the birds down and perhaps causing them to abort their migration. Would they go south on time in early October this year or would they at least go south if forced out of the high country by winter? It was finally time for us to find out.

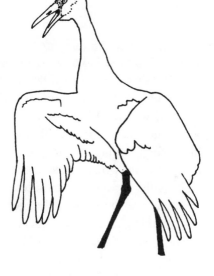

Chapter 12

Fall of the Faltering Flight

October came with no indication that our five survivors had any intention of leaving Mormon Lake, so Mormon Lake left them. As luck would have it, 1995 was Arizona's driest year in the 20th century and 1996 was not much better. By late summer, Mormon Lake had turned into one vast mud wallow. Each day coyotes and piscivorus birds gathered to scoop up the marooned minnows, and each night found our cranes increasingly vulnerable to predators. There simply was not enough water left to provide an adequate roost for the cranes. So at length, they went south . . . but only two miles. They began roosting in an artificial pond near Mormon Lake Village.

But the cranes were vulnerable even here and Dennis disappeared. For a few days, she was just missing, then on 22 October, we found Dennis, but only a head and one leg remained. Mormon Lake was becoming more dangerous, and with October mostly gone, I made a decision: we were going to "jump start" the migration and move our birds to Garland Prairie, the exact starting place of last year's migration. With a little difficulty, we herded the cranes into our makeshift welded wire trap, loaded them into the cranemobile, and by 9:30 a.m. we were on our way to Garland Prairie.

Throughout the day, the four survivors just lazily wandered about on the grassy prairie. Toward sunset, however, they became alert and marched purposefully west. We didn't want to interrupt any intentional migration (even if it was on foot), so we let them pass over the ridge to the west. I didn't believe there was a roosting pond anywhere near in that direction, so just after sunset, I grabbed the telemetry equipment and walked west hoping to see them ankle deep and fifty feet from shore in a stock pond. In the fading light, I never did find them: the radio signal said they were just too far west. In the darkness, I returned to the cranemobile and found Yoshi and Dan settling in for the evening. We heated our evening meal over a crackling ponderosa pine fire, then settled in for a cold night wondering what the next day would bring.

It's 20°F at first light, but Yoshi is up checking on our birds. He returns with the news that the cranes are still far west. Batteries store best cold but function best warm, so I tuck the frigid radio receiver between my legs and into my sleeping bag. At 6:45 a.m., I realize that the receiver will not be needed. About a mile west, we see four cranes rise up over the prairie and fly to our camp.

This development presents an intriguing possibility: why not crank up the cranemobile and see if they follow. We'll see if they continue on the migration once we lose them in the forest. First we provide a little feed to hold the cranes nearby, then all three of us rush around loading equipment. Soon we have the cranemobile lumbering toward the graded road. By the time we have the flags up flapping in the wind and begin to yell our Gawooowws, the birds, about 300 yards north of us, have already taken to the air. We roar off with dust flying and hearts pounding, all of us (humans and cranes) wondering what's gonna happen next. The cranes are flying parallel with us but still to the north. Then their path converges with ours and they're slightly ahead, so who is following who? They gradually veer south and about the time we enter the woods at the west side of Garland Prairie, they circle down and land a few hundred yards to the south.

As I see it, we have done all we should to goad our birds into migrating, so the best thing we can do now is to stay out of sight and let them show us what they can do. We head for Mormon Lake to see if the cranes have beat us back. No signals, so we head south for home.

It's 24 October and only one day since we left our cranes on Garland Prairie. The phone rings and David Moulton announces that he has four cranes by his house just about where we last saw them on the prairie. I urge the use of an attack dog and charging while yelling and flailing the air with a towel or jacket. Mr. Moulton agrees to try to drive the birds away.

The days slip slowly by. Each day we review the e-mail from NASA, searching for news from the Tiros satellites that our birds have gone south. Finally, 1 November rolls around and we get a phone call, not from NASA, but from an Arizona state wildlife management officer. Four cranes have invaded an elementary school in Cottonwood, Arizona, thirty miles south of Garland Prairie. The birds are migrating! I don't know whether to shout for joy for the migration or cry over the invasion. My long time friend, Dwight Smith, a professor at Southern Connecticut State University, has flown out for an adventure, so we jump in my Isuzu and head for Cottonwood. We are racing the clock: if we don't make record time, the cranes will probably fly off to some pond to roost, then tomorrow will invade some other school. We race north in hopes we can capture the four before dark.

I turn off Interstate 17 at Camp Verde and at the top of the exit ramp see a police car passing left to right. My focus on the officer results in my not seeing a newly installed traffic signal. So right there in full view of the police, I run a red light. The cop swings around and turns on the flashing lights. It's almost sunset: I do not have time for this. I pull over and explain to the cop that this is the first time I've gone through this intersection since the new light was installed and besides, I was distracted by him. He chuckles, says he's never heard that excuse before, and writes me a warning. Very soon we're pushing west toward Cottonwood.

We arrive shortly after sunset but have no idea where the school is located. All in a dither, we drop into the first convenient gas station. I ask a patron where the elementary school is and get the surprising answer, "Which one?" I say the nearest and he begins a snail's pace monolog, "Go to the second light, turn left, that will be Mingus Road, then . . ." As soon as can be done courteously, we end the conversation and plunge into the rush hour traffic. Within ten minutes and only one or two infractions later, we pull up by a school, and yes, there are four cranes standing by a tall brick wall. A white-haired gentleman in jeans and a black silk jacket has his arms extended as if guarding the birds. I jump from the car and rush for the birds as I bark over my shoulder for Dwight to find a parking place near the cranes.

158

Next thing I know, I have taken command of the situation. I have positioned the silk-jacketed man and three kids in a semicircle, and we are herding the cranes down a grassy alley between two buildings. I know these birds too well to think that the fourth crane will let me grab it after it watches me grab its three flockmates, so we herd the four toward the open classroom. I run ahead to get permission to enter with the cranes and to reassure the teacher that the birds are probably very hungry and therefore shouldn't leave behind any deposits on her carpet. Plan A works perfectly: these kids move the birds as though they have Basque ancestry. Once the birds are inside, we rush about trying to round up safety pins and tape so we can truss up the cranes and get them on the road. One teacher produces about forty safety pins, but they are so small that I fear the cranes can burst them. Soon some tape arrives and we are ready to start the roundup.

Meanwhile the cranes have been nervously prancing about the classroom and even before we start trussing, there are ten puddles of wet brown mush on the carpet. I apologize and the teacher kindly replies that she's been "trying for three years to get a new carpet . . . maybe this will do the trick. Besides we'll just put vomit powder on it." Vomit powder? I always thought it would be fun teaching Fourth Grade . . . maybe not. Before Dwight and I have all four cranes trussed up and ready for loading, the mush puddles total about thirty. A middle aged Mexican fellow named Jesus has appeared with a box of cat-litter-looking gray powder. He is dumping a handful of it on each pile.

Not wanting to prolong the embarrassment for ourselves, I rush off into the darkness and begin preparing a bed for the cranes in the Isuzu. One-by-one, in quick succession, we cart our four very big, very angry birds to the car. As quickly as Dwight brings them, I nestle them into soft depressions for the three hour drive. Soon Dwight arrives with the fourth crane and assures me that he has profusely thanked all, so I start the engine and retrace Dwight's tracks across the lawn and playground, over the curb, then out of town. At times like these, the best I can do is hope people enjoy the novelty of what has just happened. If they didn't, then I just hope they don't have any lawyer friends.

As we drive into the night, the lights of Cottonwood, Arizona diminish, then disappear, in the rearview mirror. I realize that I never got the name of the man in the silk jacket, or the kids, or even the teachers. All I remember is that we left an awful mess, and that a man named Jesus was even now cleaning up behind me. I ponder: perhaps this little episode is a metaphor for my life.

It is three and a half hours before we will be home. By the time we hit Interstate 17, we have got trouble in the back seat. 86 has burst his safety pins and wriggled free of his trusses. Now he hulks there, legs still taped together, wings drooping for support. He seems happy to be up and doesn't struggle further, so I decide to just leave him wobbling there in the back of the car, silhouetted by the headlights of each approaching vehicle. Crossing Bloody Basin, 26 comes loose and rises up. We've got two and a half hours yet to drive, and there are already two cranes loose in the car. But the darkness acts like a tranquilizer. Still, every few minutes one or another crane flails and thrashes, and just as often Dwight repeats the mantra, "There, there, it's all right." Anxious to end this marathon, I take a dirt road shortcut, so for fourteen miles we bounce and sway, dust billowing behind us. The cranes are by now in an automobile-induced trance so little thrashing takes place.

It is only 10:30 p.m. when we bounce up the rocky lane to my house, but I'm tired enough that I make another bad decision. Rather than properly install the cranes, their food and water in the aviaries down the hill, I decide to just release all four in the pen with Lothvar, my eagle, and sort things out at first light. One-by-one we walk the cranes into Lothvar's spacious pen, introduce them to her bath, and provide a bucket of food. "Wok, wok, wok," I explain to Lothvar, assuring her that everything will be okay. Then Dwight and I hastily retreat to our sleeping quarters.

It's past dawn when my groggy mind focuses on the fact that I have four lethal bills housed with eight lethal talons in the backyard. I bolt upright, leap out of bed, and part the curtains. A strange drama is unfolding. Dwight has been up for some time and sits there in the dining room watching the face-off. 86, backed by three other cranes, stands there facing Lothvar. Lothvar weighs more than any crane, but even with her wings spread in a threat, she looks very short and very small facing the towering cranes. 86 leaps up and rakes at Lothvar with his feet, thrashes his wings, then rises to full height ready to deliver a killing stab at my precious eagle's head. In a flash, Dwight and I are out of the house, yelling to disrupt the face-off, and hustling the largest cranes out of the pen. We carry two over the wall and into the aviary.

Very quickly we return for the last two. In retrospect, I wonder if last night's mini odyssey and this morning's near mayhem have satiated Dwight's quest for adventure.

For the next ten days, I am involved in an internal debate. Thirty miles from Garland Prairie to Cottonwood wasn't a very convincing migration. Should I try again and release my JDC's (juvenile delinquent cranes) at a remote location somewhere along their training route in hopes they will avoid further trouble and better demonstrate their migratory propensity? Finally I have a decision: the quest for scientific knowledge outweighs wisdom. We're going to release the cranes.

It is 13 November, 1996 when we release our gang of four. It is a long drive for Matt Shawkey and me to the Sullivan Buttes (mile 95 on our training route south). Very conveniently for us, there is a new dirt road leading away from the gravel county road and down to the northwest corner of the buttes. Near the end of that road, there stands the foundation of a new home. No one's about, so we pass to the end of the road and off-load our precious cargo of potential pilgrims. Four stately cranes peer intently at the surrounding topography. I try to read their thumb-sized minds. Do they have any idea where they are? I think not.

Matt and I maneuver a 180-degree turn with the cranemobile and grind our way back up the hill. We stop and look back at our tiny flock. Does this group hold the secret to motorized crane migrations or are they merely four lost birds? I'm hoping the satellite telemetry unit on 86's leg will answer that question.

For the next two weeks, NASA passes along the news: 86 and his flockmates seem to like Sullivan Buttes. They appear to have taken up residence. Another less friendly source calls with news that my cranes, attracted by the carpentry crew, have taken up residence in a partially-built home near where we released them. I call the rightful owner and discuss the problem. She reports that the cranes wander all over the platform leaving brown, splat-like presents wherever they go. Further, they have hissed and thrashed and intimidated the carpenters into a work stoppage. My salvation is that I can apologize so sincerely and so profusely that nobody has the heart to sue. Why do I have to accept all of the blame? Don't people know that when a big bird is in your way you just shout, wave, and charge? What have Americans turned into? Are we so thoroughly brainwashed in the philosophy of non-offense that we no longer retain a cultural memory of how to shoo away an impudent bird?

Fortunately, I didn't actually learn of the home invasion until a few days after it occurred. By the time I made contact with the offended parties, the problem had solved itself: the cranes, probably bored by the timid builders, flew not south on migration, but east, crossing the Sullivan Buttes.

Once again we didn't have to wait for a satellite fix from NASA. A home owner read my phone number from one of the crane's radios and called to say that my birds were poking holes in her screen door and consuming all of her cat food. "Sorry." What else could I say?

On 23 November, the local wildlife conservation officer captured my four wayward cranes (which probably means he walked up to them and offered a handful of cat food) and transported them to the Heritage Park Zoo. There, they worked off their debt to society and awaited the spring of 1997 when I would try again to determine what was stored in their long-term memory banks.

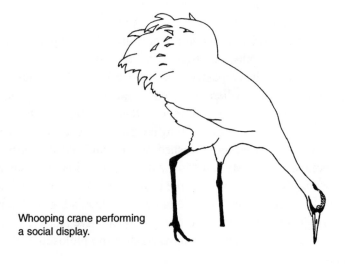

Whooping crane performing
a social display.

Chapter 13

The Sputtering Spring Migration

M arch 5, 1997. Wild cranes had been trickling north from their wintering areas in New Mexico and Arizona for three weeks, so I decided it was time to once again release the four survivors of the 1995 trucking experiment. There was some risk that they would eat more cat food and poke holes in more screen doors, but without risk, there is no gain, so I invited thirteen-year-old Sam Loveland, a budding birdman, along for a little trip to the Buenos Aires National Wildlife Refuge.

In the spring of 1996, our birds, although released each week all through March, failed to go north on their own because Mom and the cranemobile stayed stationary on the ground. Each time the cranes circled up, anxious to depart, they were lured back to earth by the familiar sights below.

In 1996, our cranes were naive and vulnerable to coyote predation so Mom could hardly leave and let them suffer a near certain fate. This year, things were different. 86 and his fellow survivors were well educated. Having endured a summer of frequent encounters with coyotes, Mom was definitely not needed.

In late winter, I recovered my birds from the Heritage Park Zoo and transported them to my home. Now it was time to move them to their spring departure site. As Sam controlled the doors, I carried the cranes, one at a time, from the aviaries in my backyard to the cranemobile. When all four were aboard, we headed for Chongo Tank, seventy-nine miles to the south. Upon our arrival, we opened the crane doors and watched 86 and his buddies one by one reluctantly and cautiously leap from the truck bed, then celebrate their reunion with the familiar waters of Chongo Tank. After a half hour whacking with my machete, I waded out into the muddy pond and erected a five-foot tall tripod of mesquite limbs. At twenty feet from shore, this would support the crane feeder and keep it from all but the most desperate racoon. My young assistant, Sam, seemed appropriately impressed with the cranes and they were delighted with their pond. I had business at the refuge headquarters, so we left our birds romping in the water.

When we returned an hour later, we crept quietly under the berm forming the pond and peeked over. All four cranes were peacefully working the shallows, so unnoticed, we slipped away. In a few minutes we were driving north, hoping that the cranes would begin their migration at their leisure now that Mom and the cranemobile were gone.

After a week, reports of crane misconduct began to trickle in. It seemed the Refuge had allowed Pima County to establish a temporary waste transfer yard less than a half mile from Chongo Tank. My four birds had invaded the yard, either for food (not likely) or in search of Mom (very likely).

On March 13, I borrowed Ben Trahan for a long lunch break and we headed south to Chongo Tank. All four cranes were present, but 86 looked dumpy. I decided it would not hurt to give him a shot of ivermectin, a broad spectrum worming agent, good for everything from African river blindness to heartworm. So we donned our crane mama costumes and circled in. By stooping low and looking away while creeping toward him, I managed to sidle close enough to lunge in and grab 86. Soon we were ready to inject. During handling, I saw that 86 had another problem, a huge, three-and-a-half-inch diameter, gaping hole across his abdomen and down onto his left drumstick. Probably the result of colliding with a barbed wire fence, it was only skin deep, but it was going to require some repair. Ben held: I dug out the suture material and ten minutes later, we released 86. He strode away, hardly limping. While Ben remedied the crane excrement problem on his hands and pants, I pondered 86's situation. He seems to be the one that attracts trouble, but he always survives: he has become the bounce-back bird.

20 March. A week goes by and it is time to check Chongo Tank again. The gang of four looks healthy, including 86, so we just fill the feeder and slip away. Will these birds ever fly north?

1 April. There has been a warm south wind blowing for two days. In hopeful anticipation of finding Chongo Tank vacated, I drive south. I find the feeder nearly full, no cranes in sight, and from the berm of the pond, I fail to detect radio signals. Elated, I drive north with my arm out the window turning the antenna right and left, listening: wouldn't it be exciting to actually detect my birds on their first independent northward migration? Then it occurs to me: this group has done so many things wrong, maybe I should be driving south into Mexico with my arm out the window. Arizona is a very big state: sans airplane, all I can do now is wait, wait and pray.

Good news! 4 April. I get another of those "guess what your birds are doing" calls from Phil Smith at the Arizona Game and Fish Department. There are four very friendly cranes at the Casa Grande Golf Course. No one has been attacked, but the operators of the golf course request their removal. As quickly as possible, I mobilize the cranemobile, snatch Sam Loveland from his home-schooled studies, and soon we lurch west toward Casa Grande.

Even before we leave Oracle, the cranemobile begins acting up. The brakes grab-and-release in oscillating harmonics with the result that we are bouncing about in the cab like a couple of basketballs. Sam is unable to believe that I am not secretly trying to make his life miserable by somehow pressing a hidden pedal or button. When it happens, and it can happen at any speed and at any time, the bouncing increases in severity until everyone on board is slumping forward trying to keep his cranium off the ceiling. The only way to interrupt these wild gyrations is to stop the truck. We pull over and stop. Then when we begin rolling again, the oscillations will either not show at all or begin again immediately, in which case I pull over again, stop, and begin anew. If I lightly touch the brake, it is almost guaranteed that the oscillations will begin, so when I push the brake, I push hard, stop completely, then start again without any brake contact.

We glide down the long declivity into the Sonoran Desert. With only four brake-bouncing incidents, we arrive in Casa Grande. Phil's directions are good, and soon we are approaching the golf course clubhouse. Bob Grainger is very relieved to see us pull in. The gang of four (cranes) is happily marching about on the lawns. We deputize four visitors and herd the birds toward the clubhouse. We outsmart the cranes into going into a corner. I whip in, pounce on 86, grasping him by the elbow (yes, cranes do have elbows), then as my other arm reaches over, I furl both wings and pull him in and cradle him against my chest. The other arm now grabs both legs at the hock. I lift the bird off the ground: his feet flail empty air as I rush him to the cranemobile. Sam controls the hasp and door until 86 is safely inside. Soon we have the other three cornered, but they skip past us and fly out into the open. One group of golfers and one guy on a bike flee as the birds come rushing by. Two more roundup attempts and we have all four birds safely in the back of the cranemobile.

By this time, we have attracted considerable attention. Hoping to avoid further embarrassment, we hasten to close up the cranemobile and slip away. But this is not to be. One of our deputy crane herders, a portly fifty-five-year-old with graying hair, sees an opportunity. Seems there was a bedraggled goose he would prefer not having around to embarrass the golf course operators. Would I please consider removing him also? My thoughts turned immediately to the needs of Lothvar, my eagle. Of course, I would be glad to remove the goose and gave assurance I could be counted upon to place it where it would be better appreciated. Sam and I turn our attention to the half dozen domestic waterfowl hanging around in the shade of the club house. There are some blotchy, Muscovy ducks, a very scruffy white mongrel "mallard," and a healthy-looking gray lag goose.

No sense wasting time, I stride purposefully toward the goose. The goose is a territorial gander, long used to pushing golfers around: it strides purposefully toward me. With head high and hissing, and with wings open, it rushes to the battle. Right out loud I say, "That will work on some, but not on me." I grab the big gray gander by the neck and wrestle him into submission. Just as quickly, the golf course employee sputters out further instructions. "No! Not that one, the ugly one." There is only one goose here, but now I turn my attention to the scruffy duck designated by my pudgy friend. There it stands on one infected bumble-foot. The other leg dangles, broken. Its nape is featherless and chafed (probably from uninvited homosexual encounters so often directed at underlings of the mallard clan). It peers at me with one good eye. The other eye is bleary and weeping. I assess the situation: lacking ten grand for veterinary fees, this "goose" would be best served by a quick transfer to the spirit world. I keep my thoughts to myself and in five seconds, this ailing anatid has been swept up and plopped down in the cranemobile with the cranes. He waddles among the pillar-like legs. The good news is that he will provide some diversion for 86 and his three buddies while we travel the sixty miles to the next stop on the cranes' migration route.

Sam and I glide along westward. Only once is our trip interrupted by the bouncing brakes. It is 5:30 plus when we arrive at an open alfalfa field about one mile north of Gillespie Dam on the Gila River. The wild cranes that use this area left over a month ago, but there is still plenty of food for our birds.

As we leave the pavement and lumber into the field, we spy an aging, dark blue, pickup truck half way across the fields. What we are about to do is going to be thought strange to all but the most well-traveled, so we bounce our way over to the pickup. Sam watches the cranes to be sure that they are handling the bumps okay. The bumps give the duck some relief from his well-stilted traveling companions.

We stop: the dust drifts slowly northeast. I step out and say hello to Patty Kuhn (rancher's wife) and a sixteen-year-old girl with hair as red as any Irish beauty. They have binoculars and are watching birds. We open the rear doors on the cranemobile and give them some very big birds to watch. They promise to inform the Mexican braceros that work these fields to not kill our still-too-tame birds.

One by one, the cranes leap from the four-foot high bed of the cranemobile. They busy themselves, stabbing for weed tubers and bugs

Whooping crane with crown expanded in social display.

amid the alfalfa plants, seemingly oblivious of our quandary over the fate of the dirty-white dwarf with the orange bill that shared their journey to the Gila River.

As fate would have it, the girl-of-burnt-umber-locks loves ducks, knows a wildlife rehabilitator, and will save Lothvar the risk of possible infection. Actually, my promise to the Casa Grande Golf Course employee was worded such that I could not have taken the duck home anyhow. Sam and I had planned on giving Mr. Duck a few days of freedom on the

167

Gila River, an intermittent stream of recycled sewer water from the metropolis of Phoenix, supplemented by chemical-laden agricultural runoff. His fate there would have been a nighttime coyote or sunlit eagle, with the conclusion no less certain than if he had traveled home with me to meet Lothvar.

We spend an hour watching our birds peck about in the fields. They seem at home. This spot lies only a few miles south of the route they flew one and a half years ago. They should find a good roost tonight, safe from coyotes, along the Gila River. I ponder their future and hope they find their way north to the marshes at Mormon Lake, far away and still frozen.

At about 6:15 p.m., the cranes become nervous and quit feeding. Their quiet gargles (i.e., contact calls) change into the more urgent pre-flight call. First 86, then the others, assume the head-pointed-forward, neck-arched-high, pre-flight posture. For a few seconds, they stand in this stereotyped posture like plastic lawn ornaments. Then 86 runs flapping into the mild breeze: all follow and the little group lifts off, circles the valley for ten minutes, then drifts east and settles into the most picturesque section of the Gila River in the region. A saguaro-studded, boulder-strewn mountain rises to the east. Wide margins of cattail line the river on both sides. Dozens of black-crowned night herons, egrets, and great blue herons will share the marsh and brushy banks with our little flock.

Sam and I move a quarter mile to the top of the volcanic bluff and watch as the group settles in for the night. At 7:25 p.m., it is too dark to see, but our radio receiver beeps stridently, telling us that our little group is still present at the wide place on the river.

Sam and I wend our way home. For two and a half hours, we bob along listening to the rumble of the cranemobile's big diesel engine. I think of how our strange experiment will be judged by the scientific world on the basis of the fate of a tiny flock dozing fitfully in shallow water as coyote and bobcat slink by, hoping for an opportunity to capture the protein equivalent of eight cottontails or three jackrabbits.

Another week goes by and on 9 April I pick up David Hancock, publisher of this book, in Phoenix. It is early spring elsewhere in America, but in this asphalt-altered environment, it is already over-hot summer. At 6 p.m., we arrive on the volcanic bluff above Gillespie Dam. I lock into place all ten arms of the five-element Yagi antenna and connect the cable leading to the receiver. Beep-beep-beep: I pick up a good strong signal from the fields to the north. It is 86, but it is only 86. Where have the other three cranes gone? I sweep wide, slow circles with the antenna, listening on each frequency: not even a quiet peep. We bounce down the bluff with the engine of my under-powered, Japanese, four-wheel drive whining near 4,000 rpm trying desperately to keep us from sprinting into some boulder. In a few minutes, we are motoring quietly across the fields to 86. I look on with alarm: a very dumpy looking crane is standing on his left leg and holding elevated a very bloody right leg. The injured leg is torn in two places. The spacing on the tears suggests he has, not long ago, perhaps last night, had a canid (coyote or dog) clamp onto his leg. He is very docile and allows our close approach. To avoid causing further injury, I decide to not grab him and from his movements, I decide that the leg, although badly scraped, is not broken. David and I stay with him long enough to see that he can fly, hop along, and land, all without putting weight on the leg. It is approaching dusk, so I decide to postpone my decision as to 86's fate until tomorrow.

This is an unexpected and shocking development. We drive off into the gathering darkness. With the three other survivors missing and 86 in a slump, the prospects are bleak. David and I wend our way westward along unfamiliar farm roads, hoping to sleep along the slopes of the Eagletail Mountains. I spot a plastic pipe on the road and save it against the possibility that we may decide to use it to splint 86's leg tomorrow. By calculation or by chance, we finally stumble onto Courthouse Rock Road and at its terminus, we see the jagged outline of the Eagletails masking our view of a star-spangled western sky. To make sure we will not be disturbed, our last 200 yards is up a wash bed and across a boulder strewn hillside. By flashlight, we locate a "flat enough" spot and gather saguaro ribs and dried mesquite limbs for our campfire. David keeps his thoughts to himself as I lay my Winchester Model 61 .22 caliber rifle on the mat between us. Around a small, but pleasant fire, we dine on canned stew and preserved fruit and discuss our plan for 86. He has survived so many injuries, it is very difficult for me to imagine him dying now.

Although it is still April, the harsh morning rays seem in a hurry to burn away the night's chill. David's attention turns to the rifle, better revealed in the daylight. I respond, "Sure it is loaded. Why would you sleep next to an empty gun?" David is from Canada where firearm use is restricted and where there is little danger of human predation. I am from the West where many are carrying guns, and I have a hungry eagle to feed. In addition, experience has shown me that a well-timed, skyward, muzzle blast can very efficiently dispel nighttime intruders including the two-legged kind.

I have always wanted to study raptors in the Eagletails, but with the arrival of morning we have a problem to solve with 86's leg. I give the cliffs above us west and south a cursory scan with the binoculars. Sign looks good for prairie falcons, but we have no time to investigate. With a cold breakfast, we are soon bumping our way down the hillside and zooming along very dusty roads back to the Gila River.

By the time of our arrival, 86 is back in the alfalfa field where he was seen yesterday. We creep in close: I decide the leg is not broken. The wound is dry on the outside and seems to be healing, so instead of splinting the leg, I creep in from behind very slowly, and spray the wound with furazolidone to fight infection. After further reflection, David and I drive off to the south and leave 86 to his fate.

But where are 51, 112, and 113? They must have left 86 at the Gila River sometime between 4 and 9 April. On 11 April, a call comes in from Phil Smith. My missing cranes have been IN the state penitentiary at Florence, Arizona. By now, I have grown accustomed to shocking phone calls about my wayward cranes, but this is the extreme. Here is the story: on 6 April, my three cranes circled down and lit in the Level 4 security zone (Level 5 is solitary confinement). The inmates, and these are the worst sort of felons, murderers and the like, were surprised and elated at the arrival of the cranes. They immediately adopted them as a gift from the skies. A call went out from the warden's office to the Arizona Game and Fish Department. Craig McMullen, the local wildlife conservation officer, rushed to Florence. This was the first time he had been in prison, so he wasn't exactly certain what was kosher in the Level 4 yard. Craig decided that the birds had flown in, so he could probably chase them around until they flew out. The cranes didn't want to leave, and Craig was getting a little aggressive in his shouts and charges. The convicts had quickly become attached to the cranes and did not like seeing them harassed. They stared at Craig with narrowed eyes. Alarmed, one of the "correction officers" hustled over to Craig, and, in a whisper, warned, "You hurt one of these birds and we're gonna have a riot on our hands." Craig blanched and scanned the shadows: the expressions and body language of the hardened men that glared at him from all around led him to a quick decision. No more chasing: we will just herd them out the gate. Three locked doors, two hallways, and two fences later, the cranes were back in the open air. Craig was not sure what he would do with them once outside, but the birds solved the problem. They trumpeted, postured, bolted, lifted off, and flew into the western sky.

A month or so later, I happened to tell the cranes-in-the-pen story to my friend, Dan Creely Jr., a man very much involved in Amerind mysticism. I asked him for his interpretation of the spiritual significance of this story. He replied, "Oh well, let's see. We have the cranes, the international symbol of peace, happiness, and long life, flying down to join a group of men who have prospects of none of these things."

When the cranes flew west into the bright Arizona evening sky, they simply vanished. If they were on Antarctica, the satellite transmitter would have detected them and relayed the message the same day. If they were on the moon, I still would have had a chance for a radio message. As the weeks went by, my assistant, Dan Mummert, and I searched the cranes' probable route across the desert floor west of the penitentiary listening for signals from the three missing birds. When 112, 113, and 51 flew west into the sunset on that April evening, they flew either into oblivion or into legend.

Chapter 14

The Final Chapter

S unday, April 13, my wife Cathy and I made a post-sermon run to Tucson to return David Hancock's shoes before he flew away. It was only fifty-five miles more to the Buenos Aires National Wildlife Refuge, so we took a second "Sabbath day's journey" to retrieve the crane feeder still at Chongo Tank.

April is late spring in the Arizona desert, so it is pleasant to see the verdant response to the winter rains. Lupines stand in long lines at the road edge, a blue regiment warning drivers to not stray left or right. In the desert, each place of perennial water is a focal point for life, deciding which species of wildlife will live. Oh, some species like the banner-tailed kangaroo rat can live for months using only "water of metabolism," water derived from oxidizing carbohydrates into carbon dioxide and water. For all others, the fickle heavens decide life or death. In the desert, a long journey at midday can yield few interesting wildlife observations, but wherever water stands, life congregates. The last two hundred yards of the approach to Chongo Tank is on dirt. We choose to leave the car on the pavement and slip quietly through the mesquites, then peek, predator-like over the rim and see what surprises await us. About fifteen small "peeps" (i.e., sandpipers) are probing the muddy shoreline on the far side of the pond. A black-necked stilt, well on his way north but still a thousand miles from his summer home, wades near the south shore. Detecting no other wildlife, we emerge onto the bank. As I approach the tripod and feeder, the stilt bleats out its warning and flies within twenty feet of us. We proceed: he retreats, then approaches again. It is unimaginable that this bird is defending a pond in the Sonoran Desert as a breeding territory, but we enjoy his pugnacity nonetheless.

I slog about in the very sticky mud retrieving the feeder from its tripod support. There comes a flood of memories from the days spent camping with Roark Trahan on this shoreline in March a year ago. So much effort went into those wonderful gray birds. The peeps are probing the shoreline: the stilt adds his life to the setting, but to me this place will always be empty without the cranes.

With the gang of three gone and likely never to return, our remaining hopes for a northward migration lay with 86, a very wounded 86. April 17 is warm and sunny as spring progresses into summer in southern Arizona, but the day carries a drafty chill for me. At midday, a telephone call comes in: 86 has invaded Arlington Elementary School. No one was hurt, but please remove him as soon as possible. Arlington is a little settlement about eight miles north of Gillespie Dam. Perhaps 86 tried to leave on his northward migration, but his ailing foot forced him down after only a few miles. Arlington is also about 160 miles from Oracle, so I am not going to arrive any time soon. I hang up. This project long ago taught me that it is pointless to plan your next move. The cranes do that for you. What should I do with 86 . . . bring him to Oracle, return him to Mormon Lake, return him to the fields by Gillespie Dam? I decide to decide while I am driving. My car is basically packed, so with only a few minutes for throwing in additional gear to cover all possibilities, I lumber down the dirt road from my home to the pavement a quarter mile away.

Once on the open highway, my concentration is no longer needed for maneuvering traffic. My thoughts take a long journey: what to do about 86? He is a survivor, but how much help will he need to survive this? How can I make a decision before I even see him? Perhaps his leg IS broken. Then what should I do? If I take him back to Oracle where I can best care for him, he will probably struggle to be free of the aviary and hurt himself more. He has survived his injury at Gillespie Dam for several days. If I return him the short distance there, no further trauma should result, but I already know he has tried to go north, so likely he will go again. Even without seeing 86, it is shaping up that I should do the longer, less-convenient trip to Mormon Lake. 86 survived the coyotes in 1996: he should know to move out in the water and survive again. I have a decision.

I have passed Arlington Elementary School dozens of times without really noticing it. It is a fenced compound with a few live-in attendants. I arrive after business hours, but there are still a half dozen kids playing on the grounds. Nordic blonds play alongside dark-eyed, black-haired kids of Mexican descent. The only thing novel here is the crane guy, so the kids gather. I discover that 86 has been locked in the janitor's closet in the school. A plump, but handsome ten-year-old rushes to a house in the compound and procures the key. Soon 86 is out of the very soiled closet and hobbling about in the bright classroom. He is showing remarkable forbearance, tolerating too many kids, way too close. I try to be cheerful to encourage the youngsters to appreciate wildlife, but it is not easy, for I very quickly discover that 86 has a broken leg. Fortunately, it looks like a greenstick break with no rotation and no lateral movement.

The first job is to immobilize the crane and get him in the car. I deputize my pre-adolescent entourage and very quickly, very gently wrap 86 in a bath towel, pin the towel in place so he can't flap, then nestle him on the front passenger's seat with his legs dangling in the foot well. He is positioned so he can flail at will without striking any hard object. He obviously doesn't like the situation, but he is not frantic: he seems resolved to his fate as if aware that his journey will soon be over.

All roads are paved for the 150 miles toward Mormon Lake, but it is very late and I am slapping myself to stay awake. As I enter the ponderosa pine forest south of Flagstaff, the signs warn of elk on the highway. Two in the barrow pit alarm me, so I am wide awake when I see the 800-pound animal in my headlights. Light pressure on the brakes and a slow left swerve sends Mr. Elk past my starboard gunnels without putting 86 in my lap.

It is nearing midnight as I approach the Mormon Lake cutoff (a saving of about forty-five miles). In a few more miles, I lumber up to the locked gate, and give heartfelt thanks for being blessed with a Forest Service key. Like a deer transfixed in the headlights, I fiddle stupidly with the lock, sheltered out of harms way in a welded steel box. I just want to go to bed and now I discover that some cursed moron has put his lock around, instead of through, the Forest Service lock. This gate would not open if I were Smokey himself. In righteous

174

indignation, I try a Smokey-like tactic. From under the driver's seat, I procure a mid-sized wrecking bar. For the next ten minutes, I set metal against metal until I am certain that permanent damage has been done to the lock placed by Mr. Moron. In earlier years (or earlier hours in the night), I would have asserted my rights more convincingly and completely, but, subdued by the need for sleep and a desire for Smokey to remain my friend, I resolve to just go around. Back in the cab, I gurgle a few reassuring calls to 86, then get my truck turned around and back on the road.

In the dead of night, I lumber down the boulder-studded hill to the place where my assistant Dan Mummert and I plan to rendezvous. Dan's big jeep reflects my headlights, a silent beacon reassuring me that we are still on Plan A. Dan is sleeping nearby, but he has already prepared a pen, a net draped over a small ponderosa pine and anchored with rocks around its perimeter. When I arrive, 86 is resting contentedly on the seat, so I decide to let him remain in the car until morning. I check the time: it is 1:30 a.m. when I plop my sleeping tarp, mat, and bedroll on the frozen ground. With sleep creeping over me, it is very difficult to get undressed before collapsing into my bag.

After a late night, I would love to sleep until the sun warms the morning. Two things recommend otherwise. When dawn comes, 86 will begin to struggle and perhaps hurt himself, and last night Dan informed me that his Jeep, although near, was buried to the axles in the muddy ground, sodden with melt water from a big snow bank above camp. We have got to move quickly to get 86 into the pen so he can recover somewhat before we release him and we have got to get Dan out of the frozen mud before the ground thaws.

Just as the sun touches the eastern horizon, we begin to scramble. First, 86 goes in the pen: he balances rather well considering he is standing on one leg and recovering from a half day's confinement in a bath towel. In an instant, I scrape and shake the frost off my sleeping gear, then jam the cranemobile into four-wheel drive and hustle into the field across the fence from Dan's car. We tie our towing straps together and in only half an hour, we have Dan safely beyond the mudhole.

We turn our attention to 86. The mud holes recommend that we walk to the lake, only about one mile away. I carry the warm, snugly crane (thirteen pounds) and Dan, the gentle giant (6 feet 4 inches, 230 pounds) carries the cold and awkward feeder. 86 strains at my arm and flails a little but mostly just gurgles. I gurgle back. From working for many years with cranes, we have learned that even poorly mimicked gurgles help tranquilize our big birds.

Once at the lake shore, we position the feeder, and I set the crane where he can hop to the feeder and, come evening, flutter out into the water to an anti-coyote depth. 86 recognizes his setting, rallies, looks very alert, and thereby provides my heavy heart with some encouragement. As we walk away leaving him there on that lonely shore, he shrinks to tiny dimensions. A chilly breeze ripples the lake surface.

Dan promises to check regularly on 86. My travels take me to Colorado, then home to Oracle. Two days pass, then Dan calls and shares the news. He found 86 floating in the shallow water not far from the crane feeder. His leg is broken, twisted, and displaced. He seems to have puncture wounds on his head.

I have seen cranes fall from collisions with powerlines and from disease. But, all those experiences were minor tremors compared to the quake I now feel. No matter what the future holds, no matter what joys or tragedies come, I doubt that I will ever feel the blow that accompanied the loss of 86. So often he had risen, Phoenix-like, from each of his sicknesses and injuries. I long ago began to believe he was charmed: he would always be there. Although he never really seemed to like me, or anyone else, I loved him. Perhaps this is the tragedy, the fatal flaw, in all of us: we cannot restrain ourselves from loving, even when the object of our affection will never, can never, return our love. On further reflection, this willingness to love without expectation of reward is not the tragedy in us, but rather a glimmer of the divine.

Shaken and humbled, I quietly ask Dan to save his body in a cool place so I can examine it. A few days later, I arrive in a late-season snow storm. Dan and I examine the carcass. My guess is that a coyote got him, but was frightened away, so nothing was eaten.

That afternoon I arrive home and extract the carcass from a cool, well-insulated bundle in the car. Before disposing of the carcass, I pull about fifteen large flight feathers from his left wing. I vow to save these and to always carry one with me when I work on any future crane reintroduction projects in Arizona. I bundle the feathers in a clear plastic bag and suspend it on my office wall. I take one secondary, slip a brass cylinder over the calamis, and suspend it from the ceiling in my car. 86 will not be forgotten.

Epilogue

With the death of 86, no birds survived from the 1995 migration. The death of 86, however, was not the end of the project but merely the closing chapter in our first expedition. As stated in the preface, there was a second migration in 1996. From this, twelve birds were released along the Gila River. These birds fared better. Although they wintered in that predator-rich environment, they stayed closely associated with wild birds, and all survived until spring. At least eight survived their second winter (1997-98). All traveled north come spring. As radio transmitters expired, we lost track of some, but at least five survived until April of 1999.

From the motorized migrations, we found that leading cranes long distances was feasible at least in unforested areas. We experienced 100% survival during training, good survival on migration (86%, 19 of 22 birds survived their training flight south). From the lessons learned in 1995 and 1996, we anticipate even greater success in future experiments.

In the final analysis, motorized migrations must be judged not only on the basis of survivorship during the training flight south, but mostly on the ability of trained birds to retrace the route. Some of our 1995 birds obviously knew the way back north for two of them, following an eagle attack, returned eighty miles to the start of the route. Others in our 1995 flock made good progress north and south at the appropriate season but had to be interrupted and translocated for bad behavior.

Our 1996 survivors, exhibited better behavior and so were given more migration opportunities. All survivors from the 1996 migration have made one or more migrations without our assistance. Sometimes a bird or two has gone to Nevada with the wild flock from Gila Bend but female cranes tend to be dispersers so this is no surprise.

It has been five years since our convulsive arrival at the Buenos Aires Refuge gate, October 14, 1995. I look back and chuckle at the anxious moments and humorous antics that attended our first trek and our second. I also look back and express deep gratitude that on neither expedition was a person injured or a vehicle severely damaged. Of the twenty-two cranes that began the migrations, only three were killed.

Looking toward the future, I wonder who is the brave (or foolish) soul who, after reading this book, will continue in our footsteps. There are two tiny flocks of Siberian cranes along the Ob River in western Siberia. One of these traverses a route from near the Arctic Circle to the heart of India. I fear for my Russian friends if they dare to follow our lead, for it may be the people, not the cranes, who will fall should they attempt to lead cranes by boat for 1,200 km across Siberia, by truck for 1,600 km across Kazakhstan, then by tank across Afghanistan over the Hindu Kush and down into the valley of the Indus. Please don't try it . . . but if you do, first give me a jingle.

Additional Reading

Allen, Robert P. 1952. *The Whooping Crane.* New York: National Audubon Society, Research Report No. 3. This is the original whooping crane monograph by the staff biologist for the National Audubon Society.

Clegg, Kent R., James C. Lewis, and David H. Ellis. 1997. Use of ultralight aircraft for introducing migratory crane populations. *Proceedings North American Crane Workshop* 7:105-113. Scientific account of the first ever ultralight-led crane migration.

Doughty, Robin W. 1989. *The Return of the Whooping Crane.* Austin: University of Texas Press. The most recent full-sized book on the whooping crane: excellent in content and beautifully illustrated.

Ellis, David H., James C. Lewis, George F. Gee, and Dwight G. Smith. 1992. Population recovery of the whooping crane with emphasis on reintroduction efforts: past and future. *Proceedings North American Crane Workshop* 6:142-150. A recent account of whooping crane conservation.

Ellis, David H., George F. Gee, and Claire M. Mirande, editors. 1996. *Cranes: Their Biology, Husbandry, and Conservation.* Washington, D.C. and Baraboo, Wisconsin: National Biological Service and International Crane Foundation. The most recent book on the cranes of the world: it provides broad coverage on biology and conservation and is the encyclopedia of crane husbandry.

Ellis, David H., Kent R. Clegg, James C. Lewis, and Errol Spaulding. 1999. Golden eagle predation on experimental sandhill and whooping cranes. *Condor* 101:664-666. A scientific account of golden eagle predation attempts on the cranes involved in all motorized migrations.

Ellis, David H., Brian Clauss, Tuyoshi Watanabe, R. Curt Mykut, Matthew Kinloch, and Catherine H. Ellis. 1997. Results of an experiment to lead cranes on migration behind motorized ground vehicles. *Proceedings North American Crane Workshop* 7:114-122. Scientific account of the first ever truck-led crane migration.

Horton, Tom. 1996. "Final Flight/Route to Recovery." *Baltimore Sun, Sun Magazine.* 28 January. Pp. 6-10. Outdoor writer, Tom Horton, gives his account of his one-day, wild ride with the 1995 migration.

Johnsgard, Paul A. 1983. *Cranes of the World*. Bloomington: Indiana University Press. This large volume treats the general ecology of all species of cranes worldwide.

McNulty, Faith. 1966. *The Whooping Crane*. New York: E. P. Dutton. This little volume provides an old, but excellent, treatment of whooping crane biology and the politics of crane conservation.

Nagendran, Menakshi, Richard P. Urbanek, and David H. Ellis. 1996. Reintroduction techniques. Pages 231-240 in David H. Ellis, George F. Gee, and Claire M. Mirande, eds. *Cranes: Their Biology, Husbandry, and Conservation*. Washington, D.C. and Baraboo, Wisconsin: National Biological Service and International Crane Foundation. A recent summary of crane reintroduction experiments.

CRANES:
Their Biology, Husbandry, and Conservation
Editors: David H. Ellis, George F. Gee, Claire M. Mirande
ISBN 0-88839-385-7
8½ X 11, HC, 320pp

Published by: **HANCOCK HOUSE PUBLISHERS LTD.**

(604) 538-1114   Fax (604) 538-2262
(800) 938-1114   Fax (800) 983-2262
Web Site: www.hancockhouse.com
email: sales@hancockhouse.com

Bolt from the Blue:
Wild Peregrines on the Hunt
Dick Dekker
ISBN 0-88839-434-9
5½ X 8½, SC, 192 pp.

Published by: **HANCOCK HOUSE PUBLISHERS LTD.**

(604) 538-1114   Fax (604) 538-2262
(800) 938-1114   Fax (800) 983-2262
Web Site: www.hancockhouse.com
email: sales@hancockhouse.com